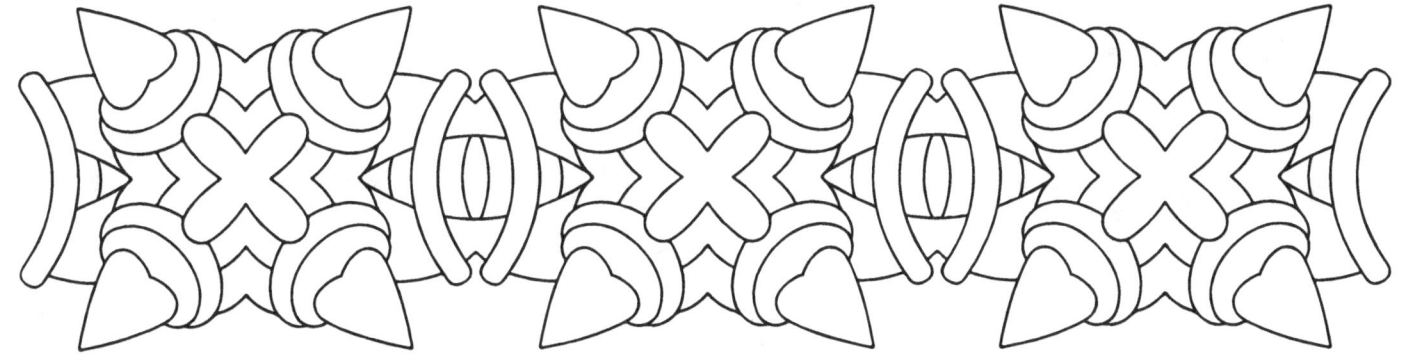

EASY
PATTERNS

Lori's Large Space Pattern Coloring Books for Adults

VOLUME 1

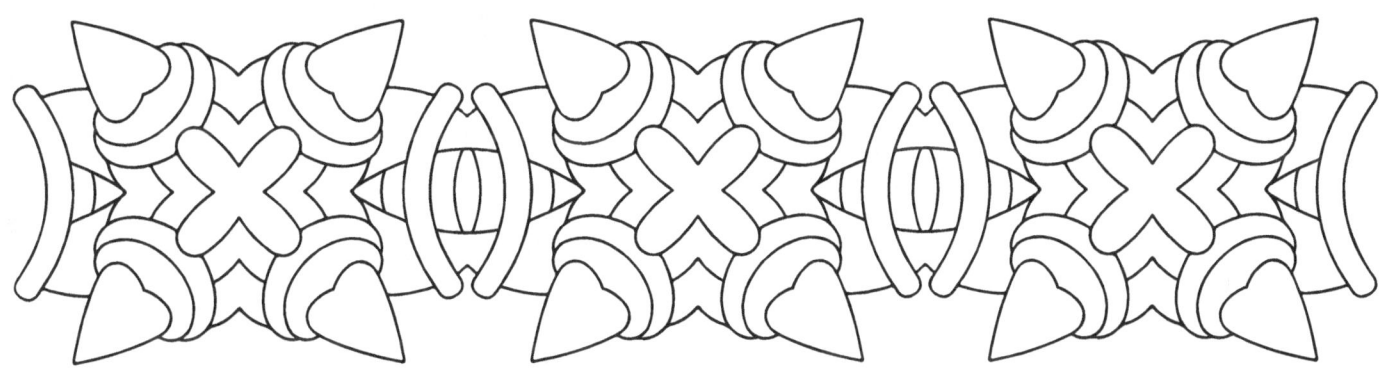

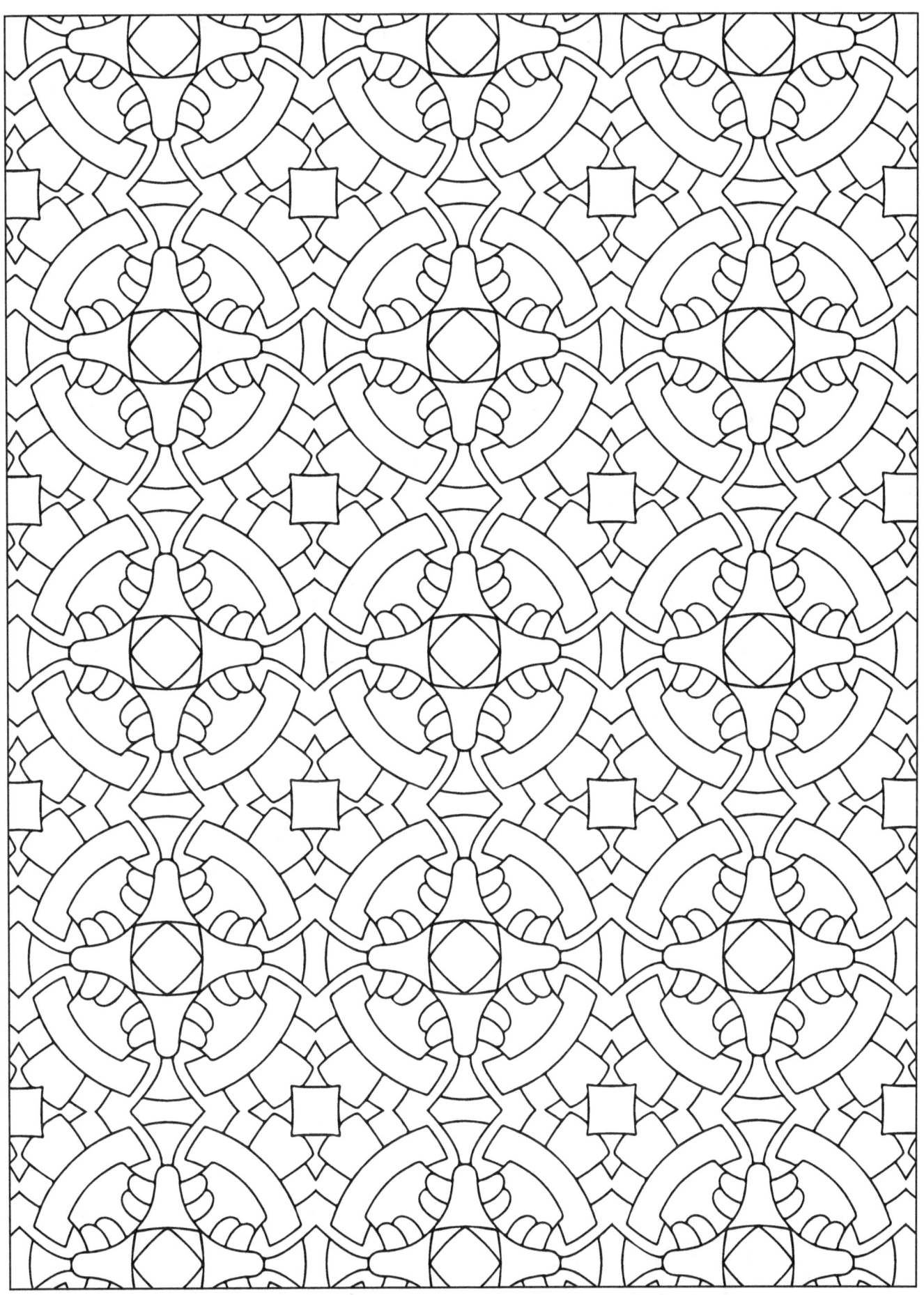

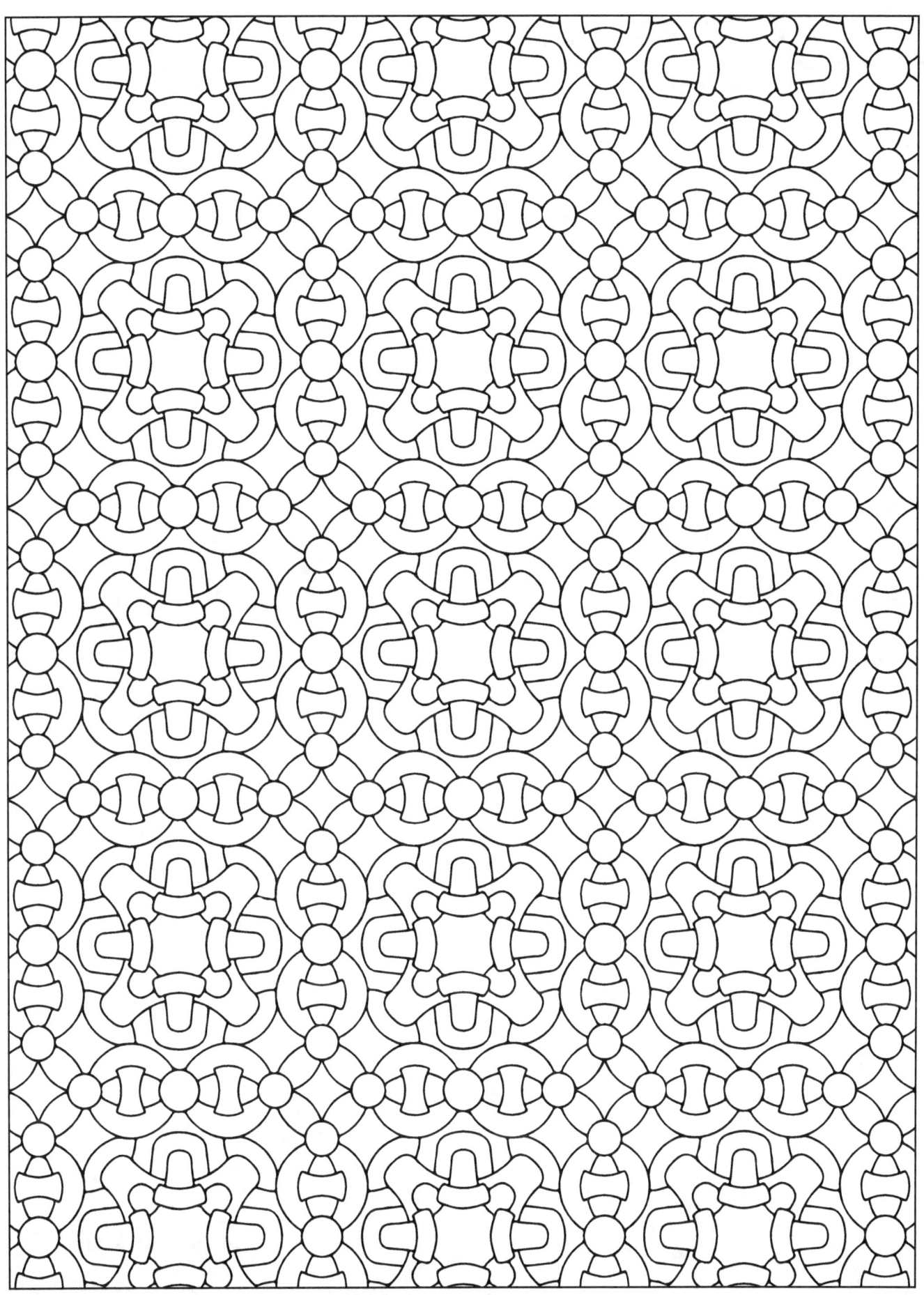

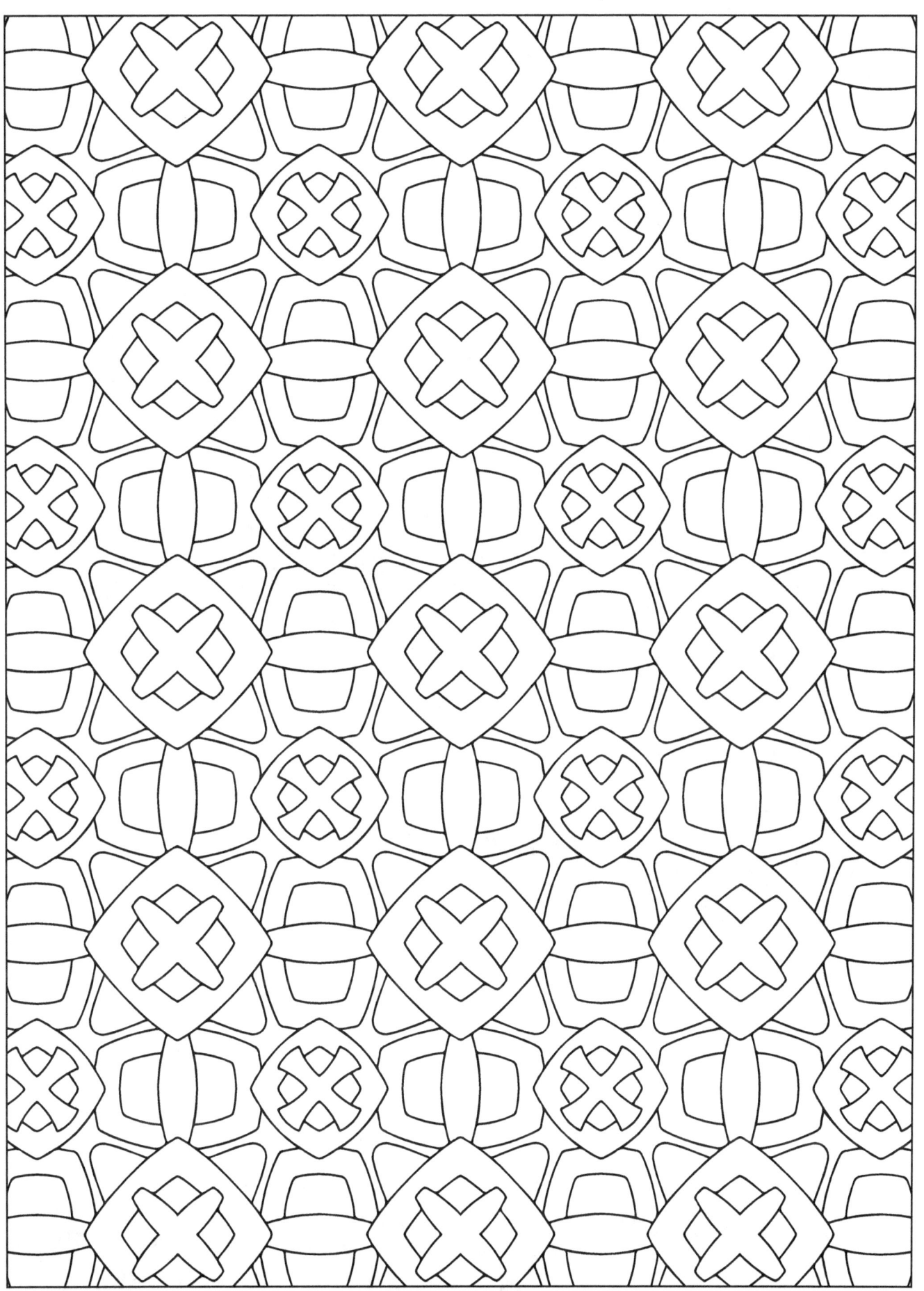

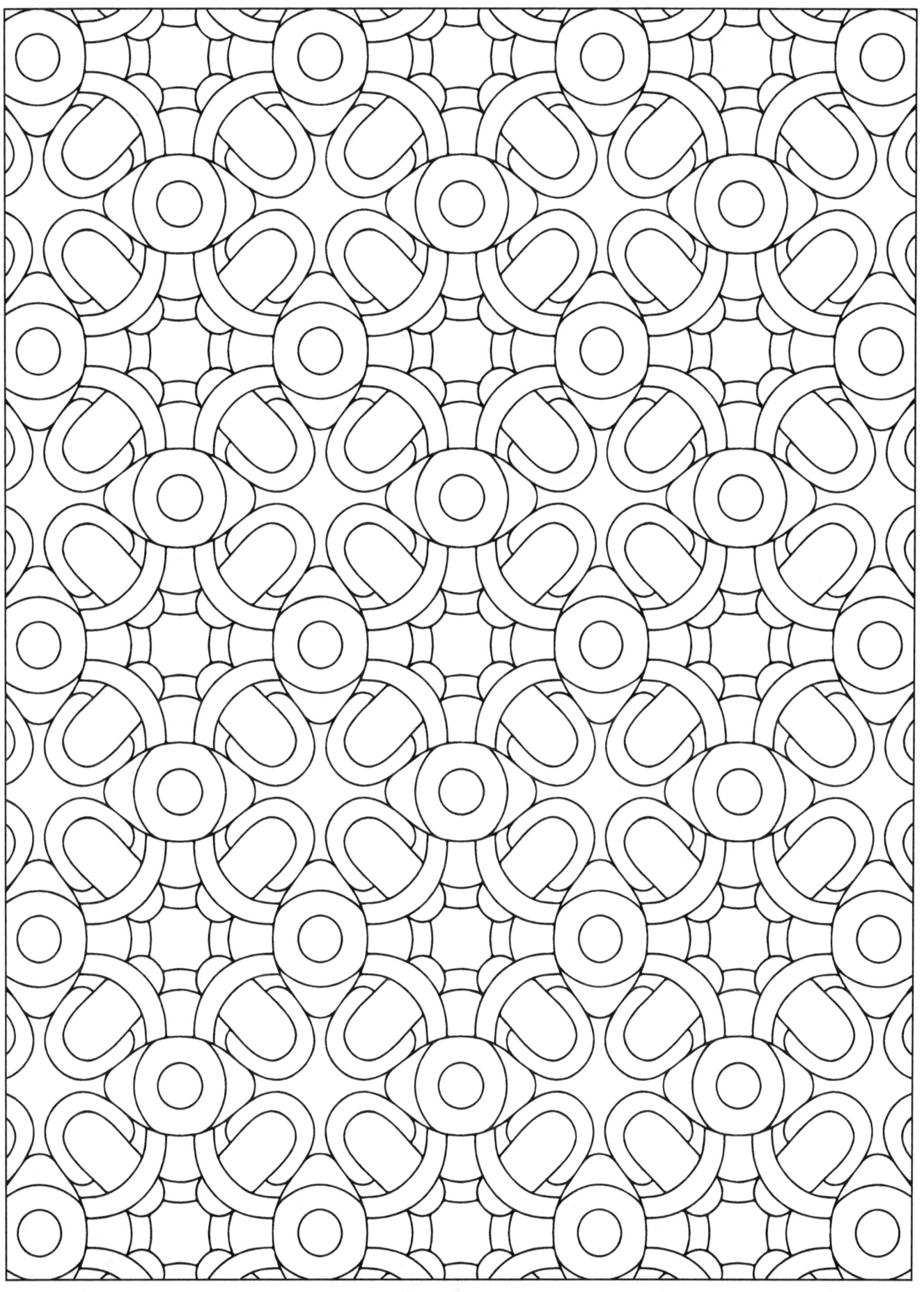

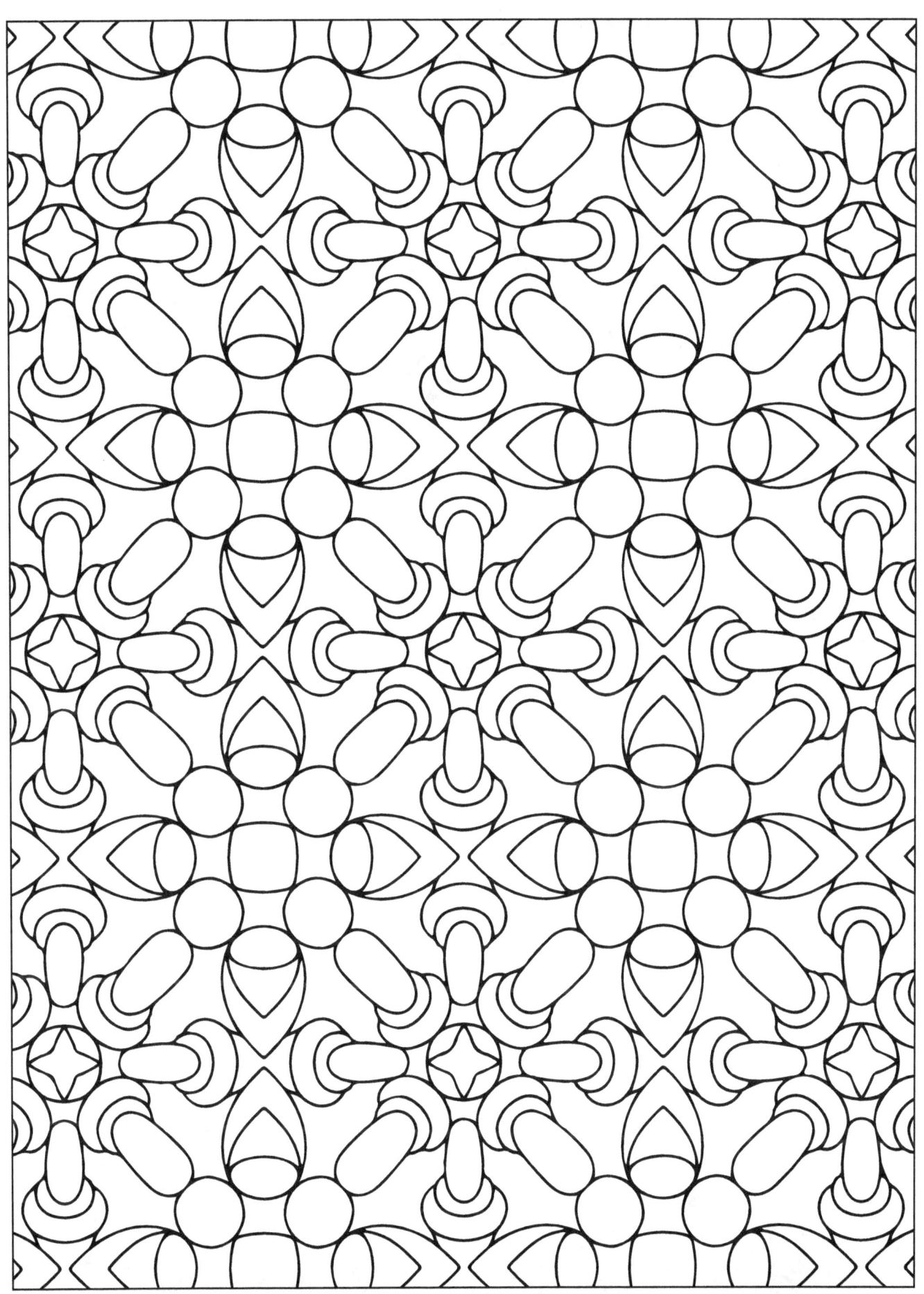

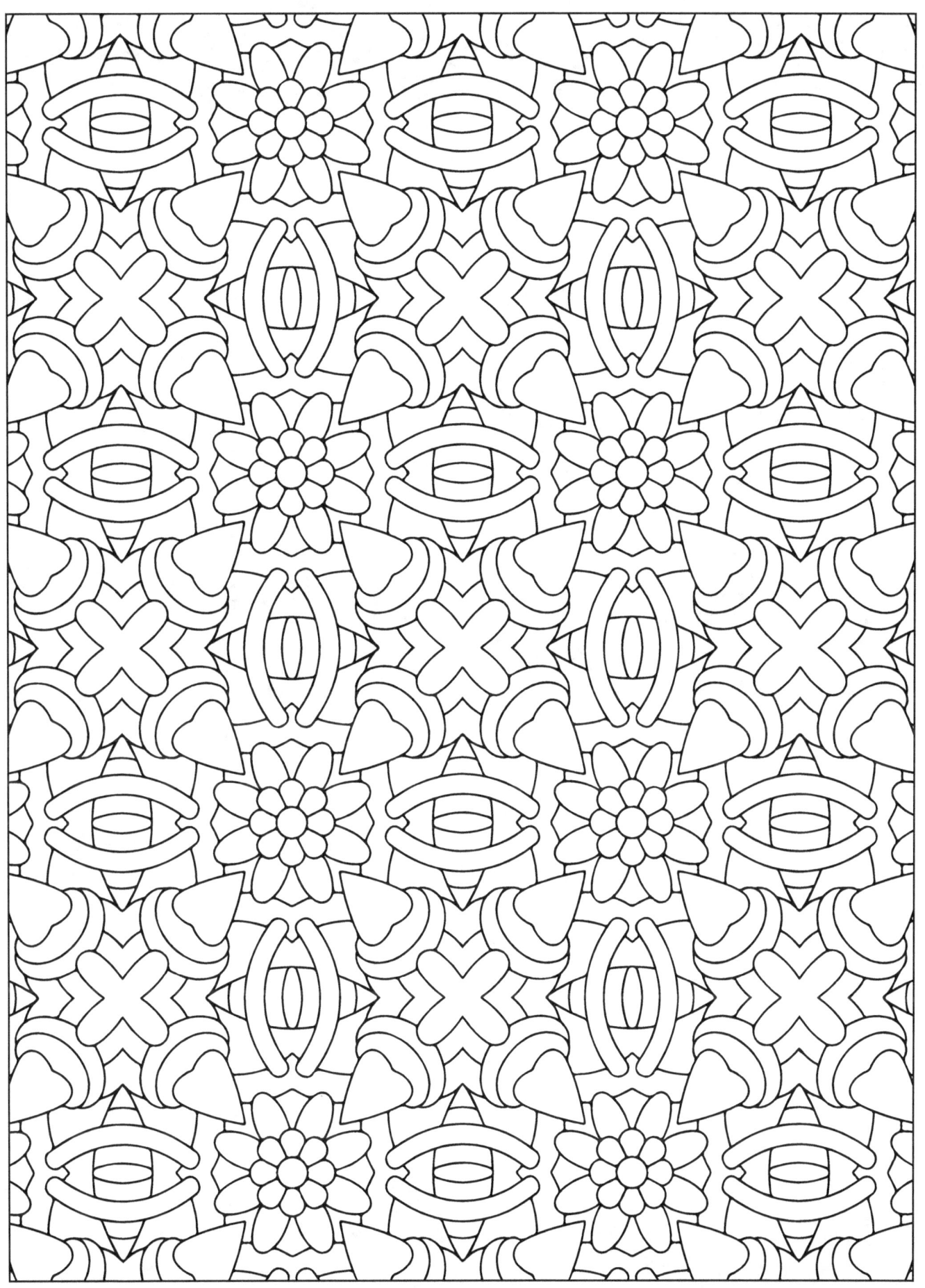

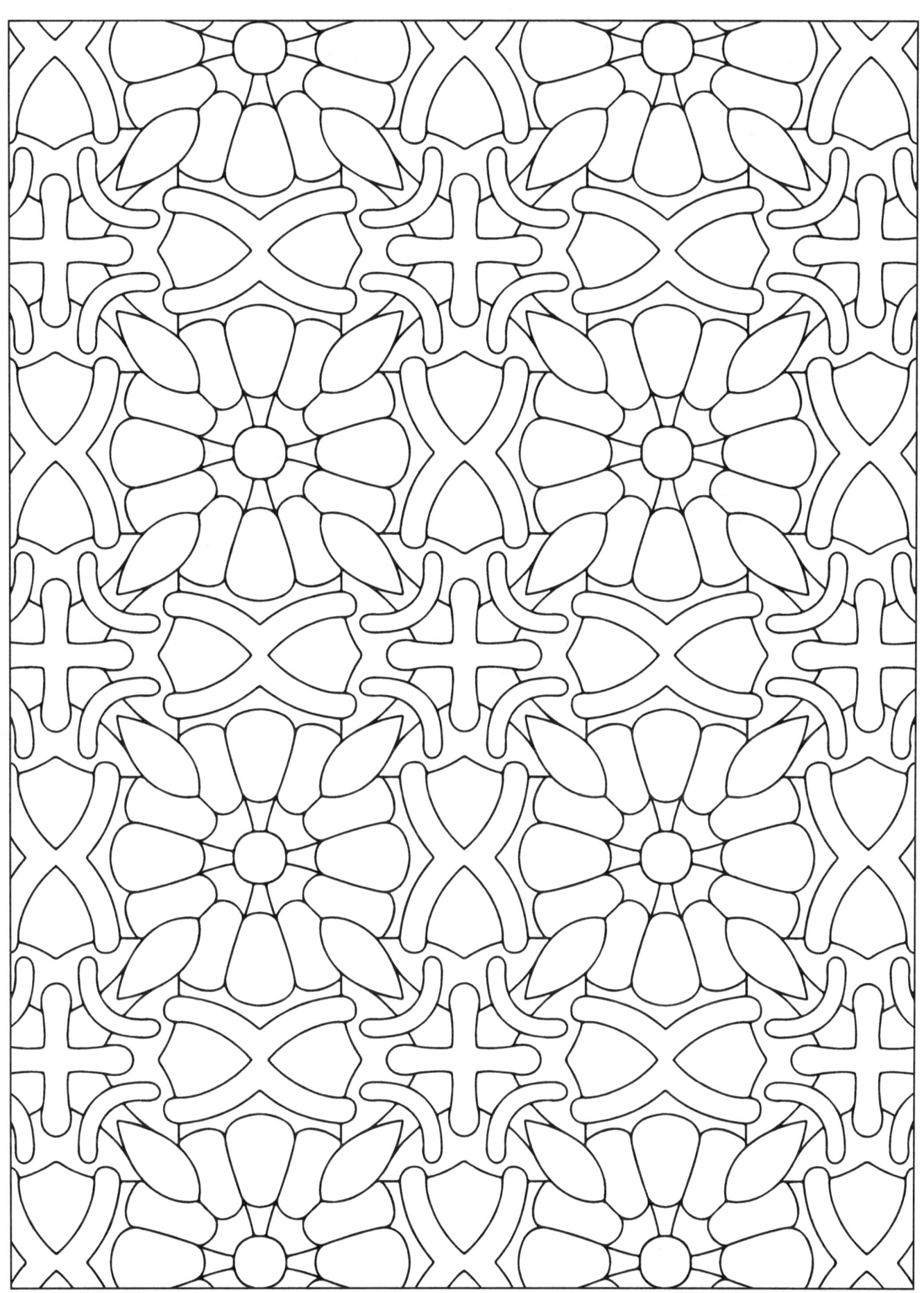

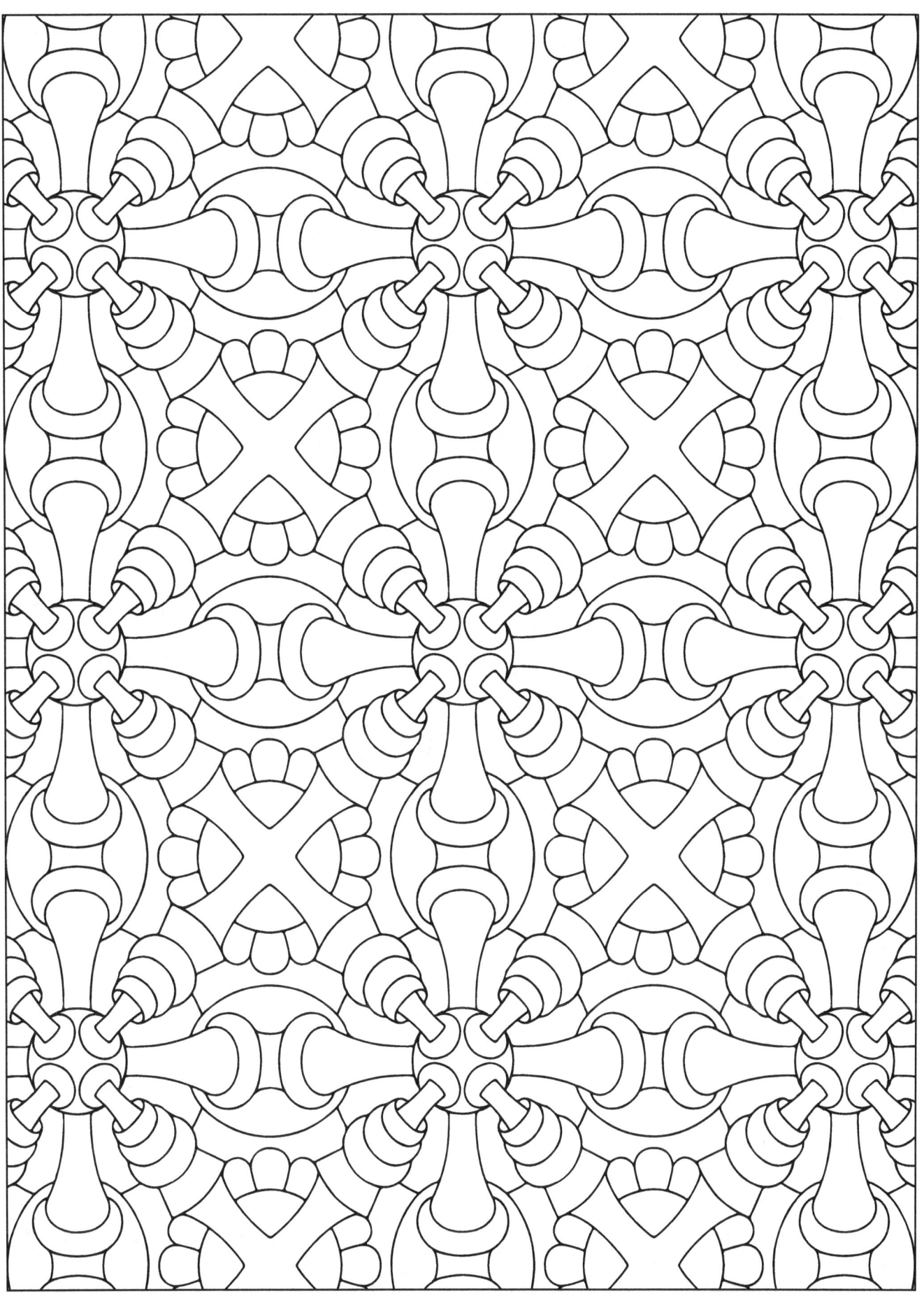

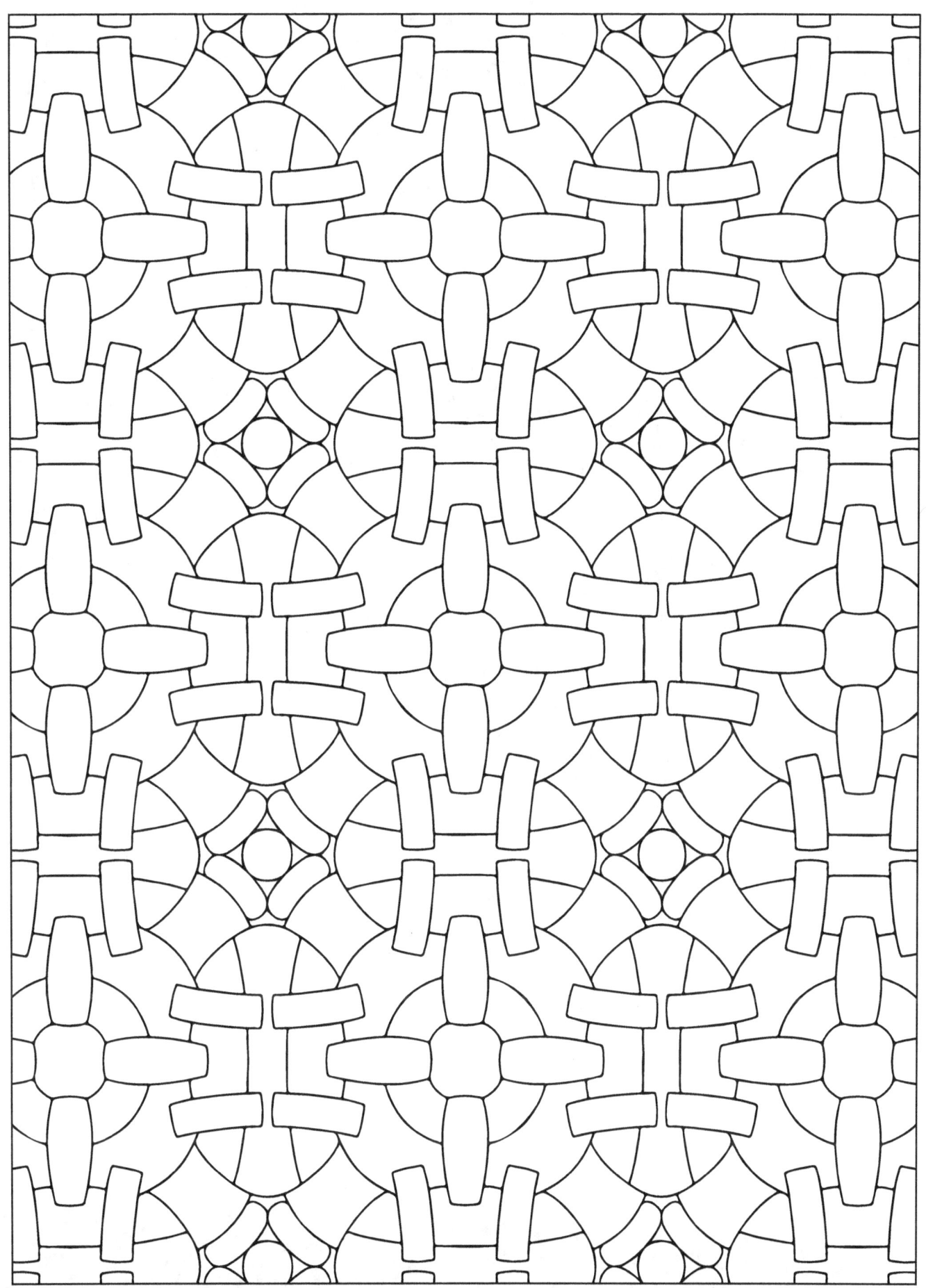

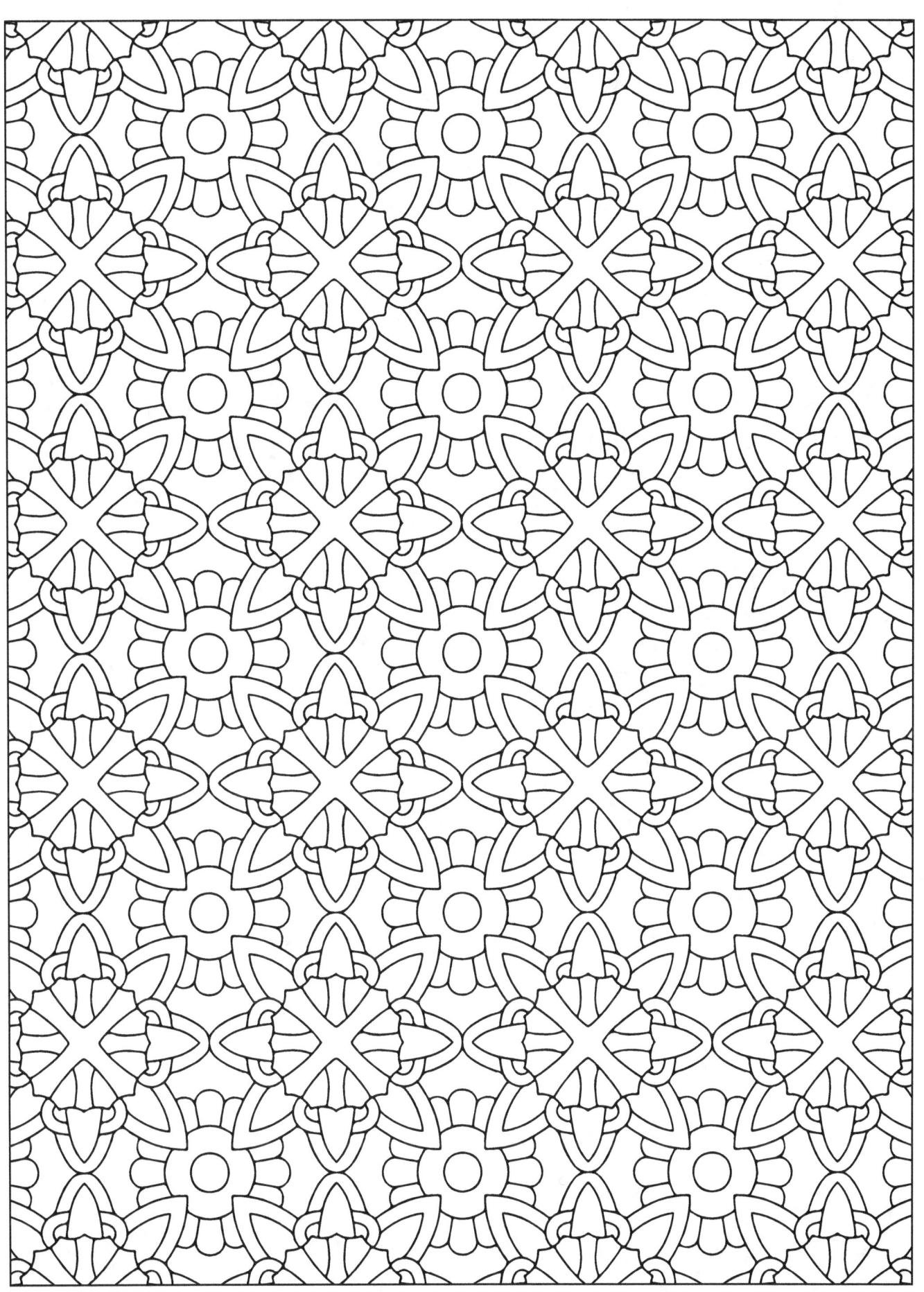

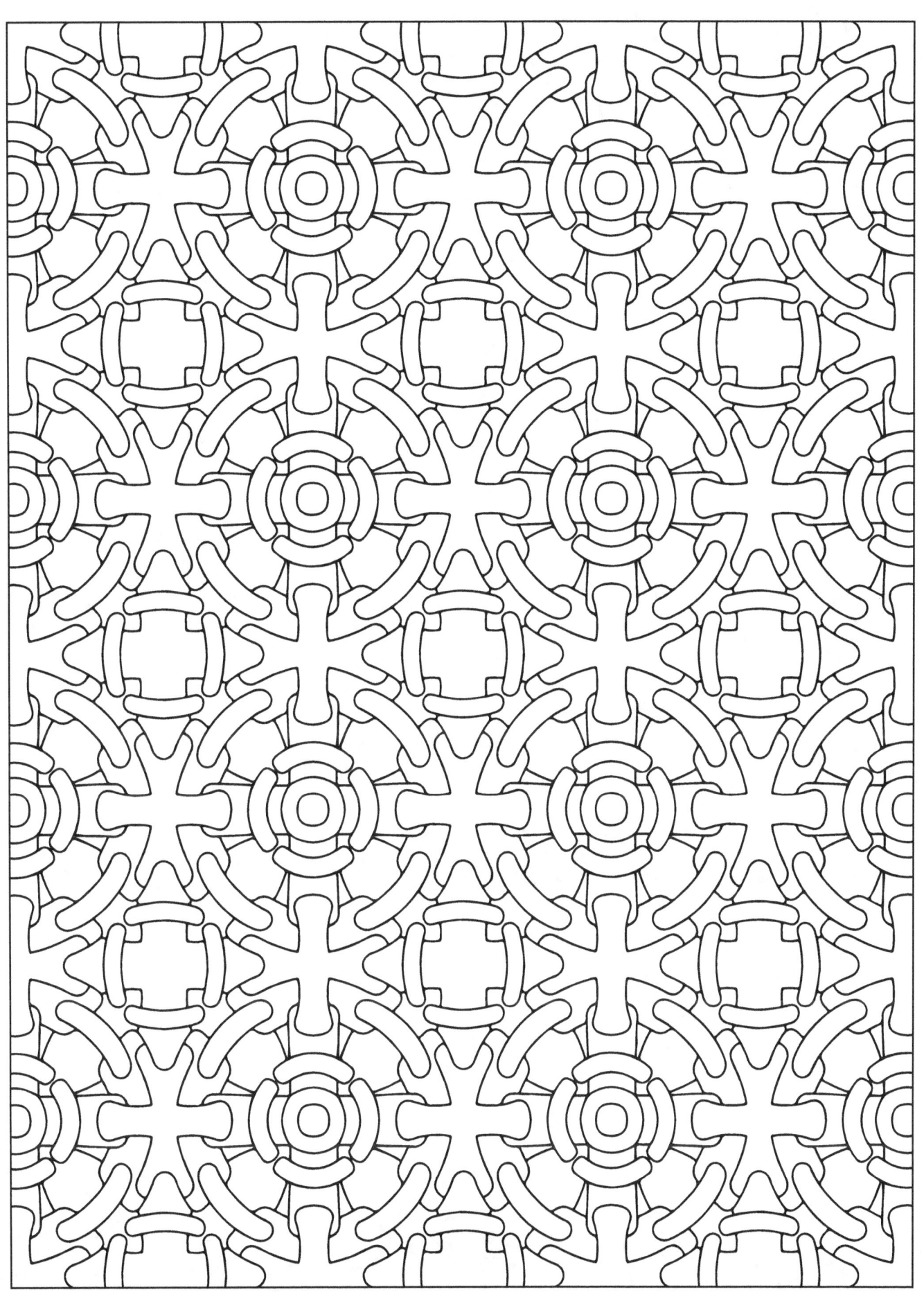

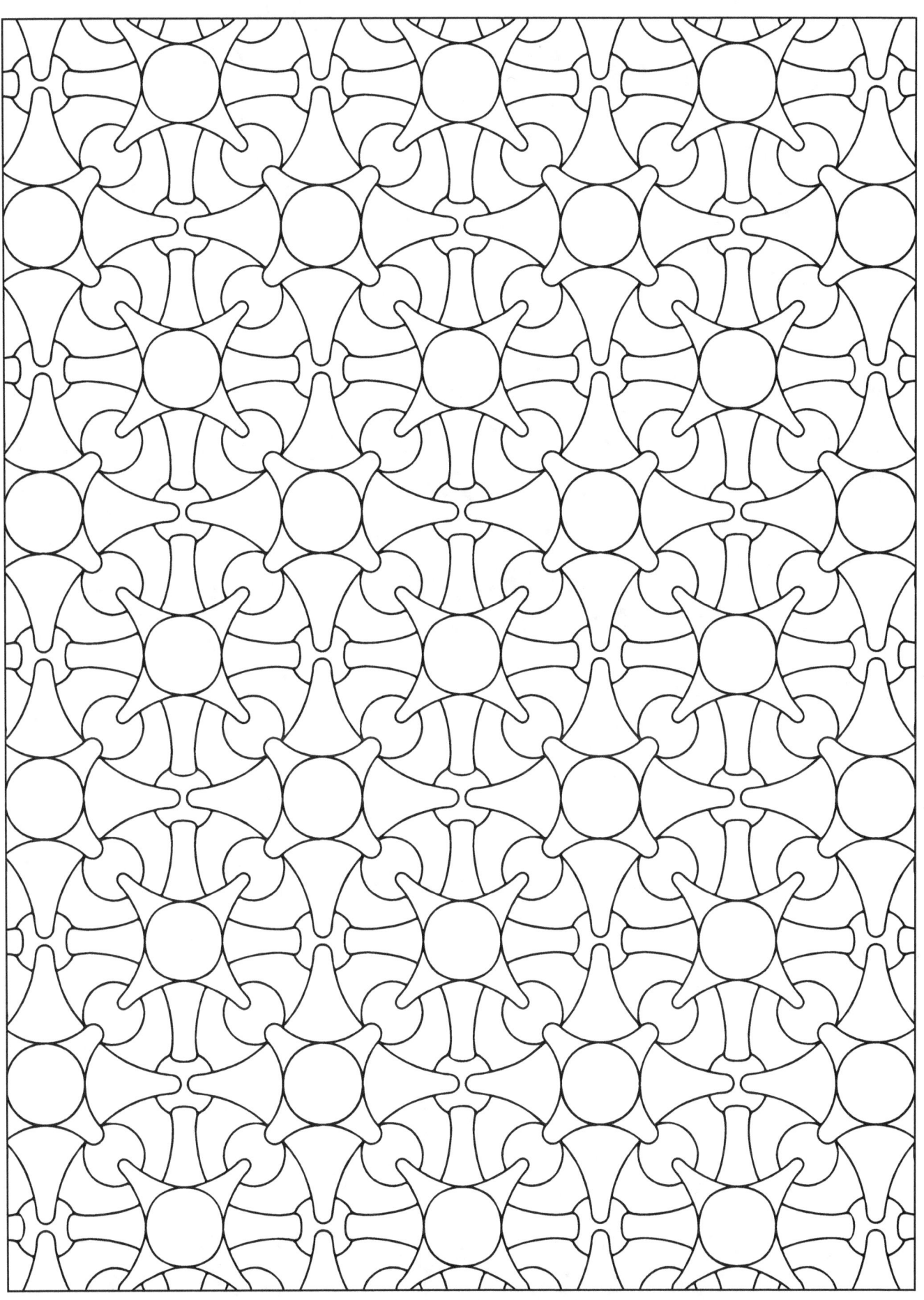

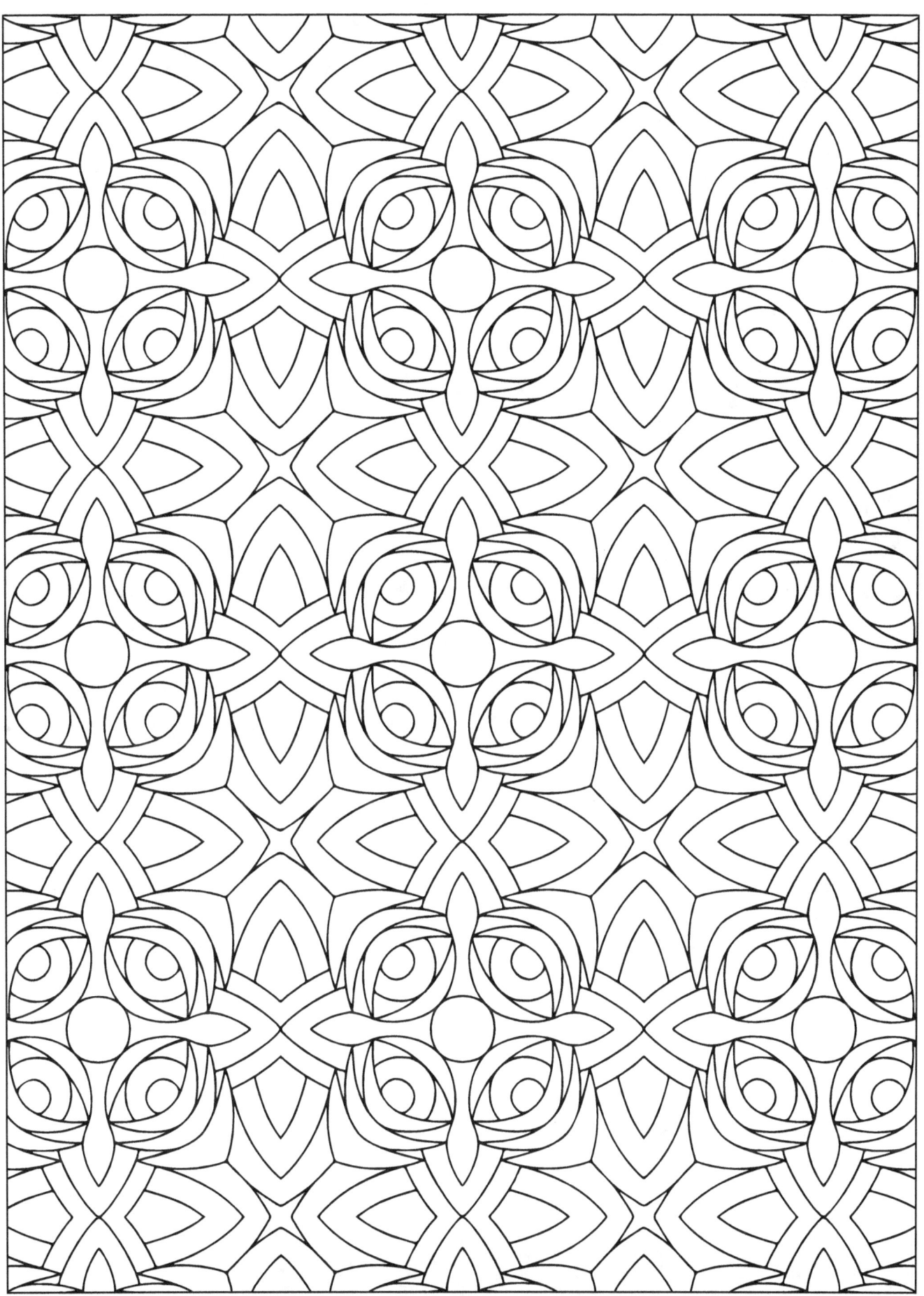

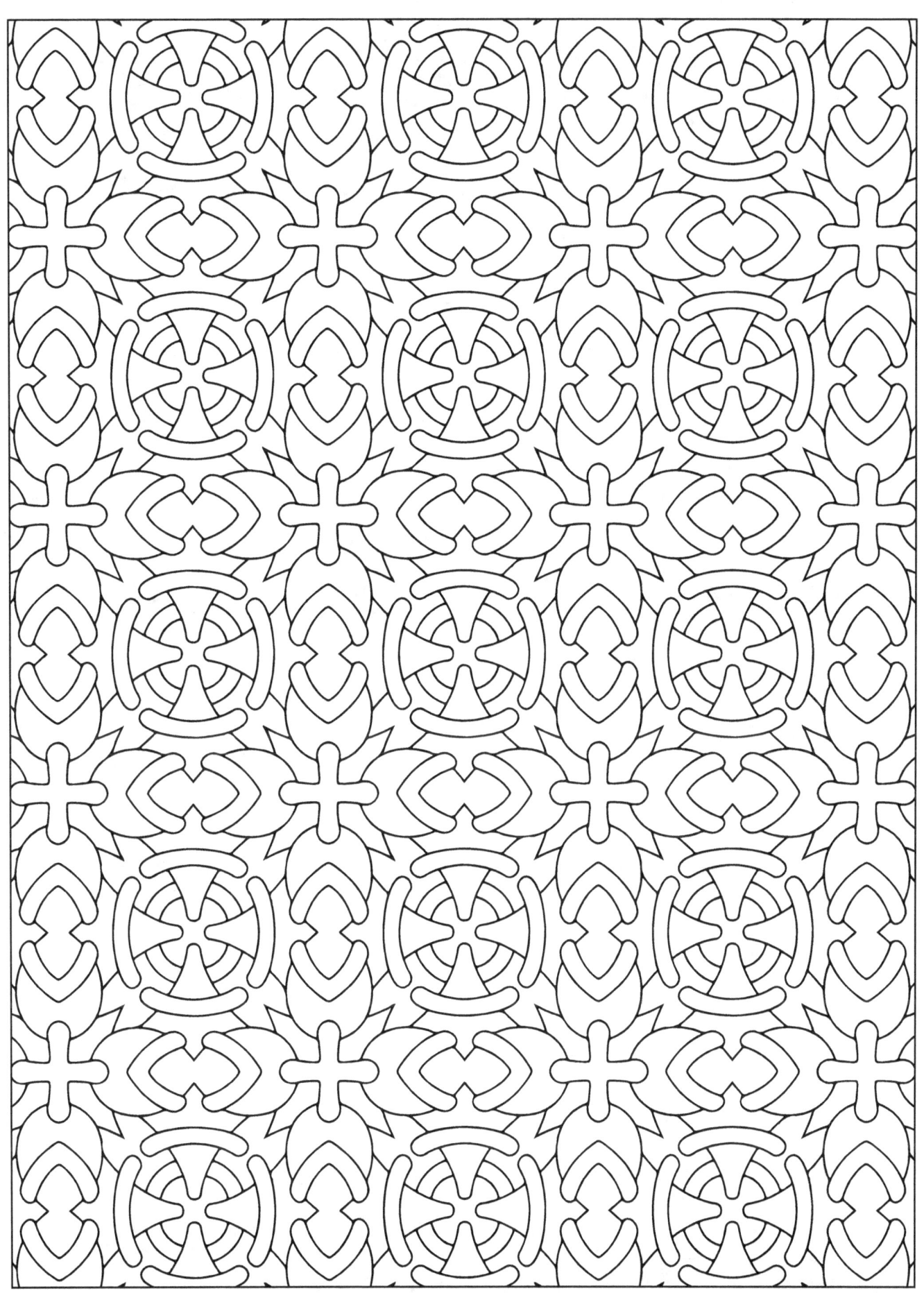

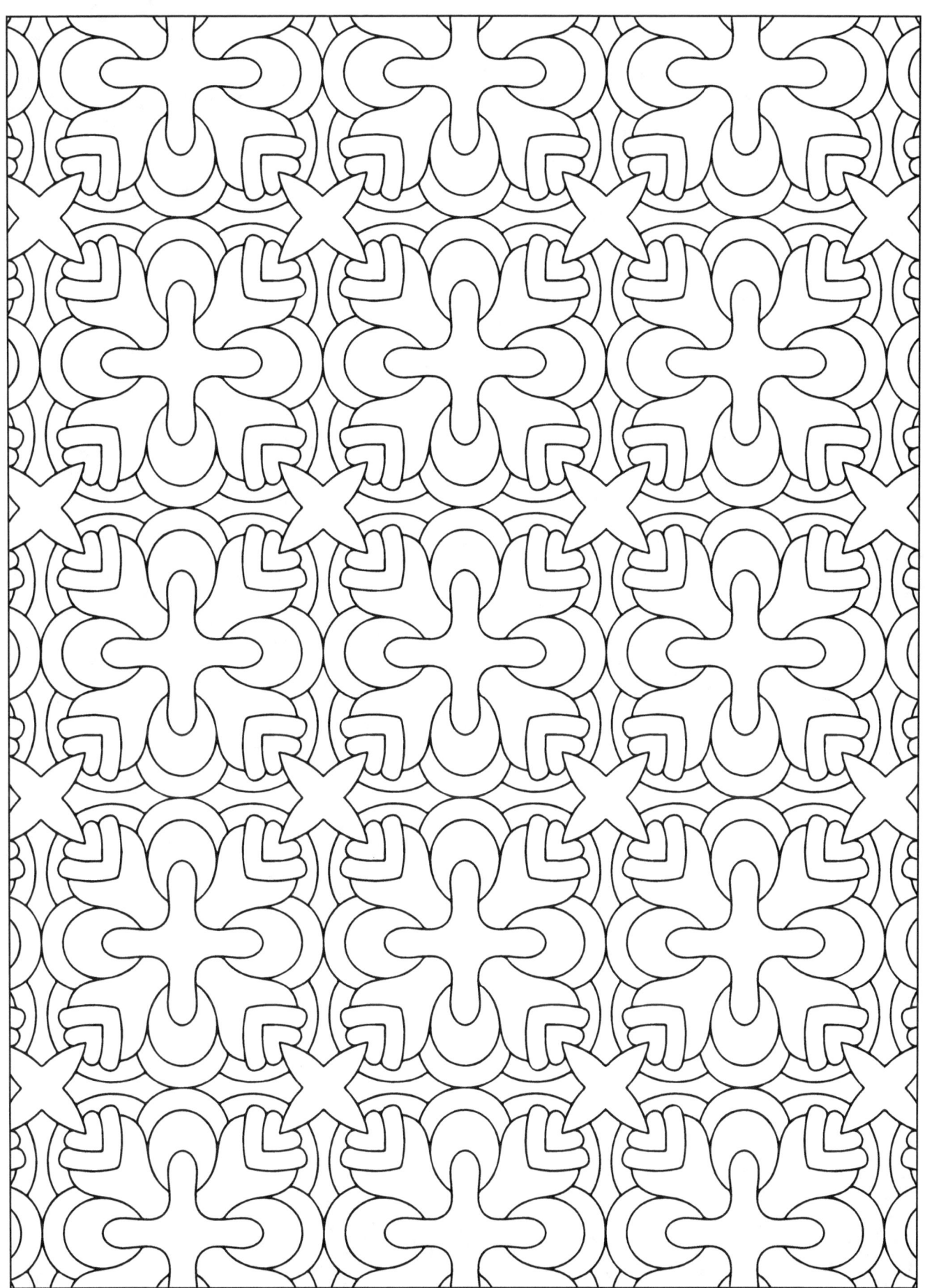

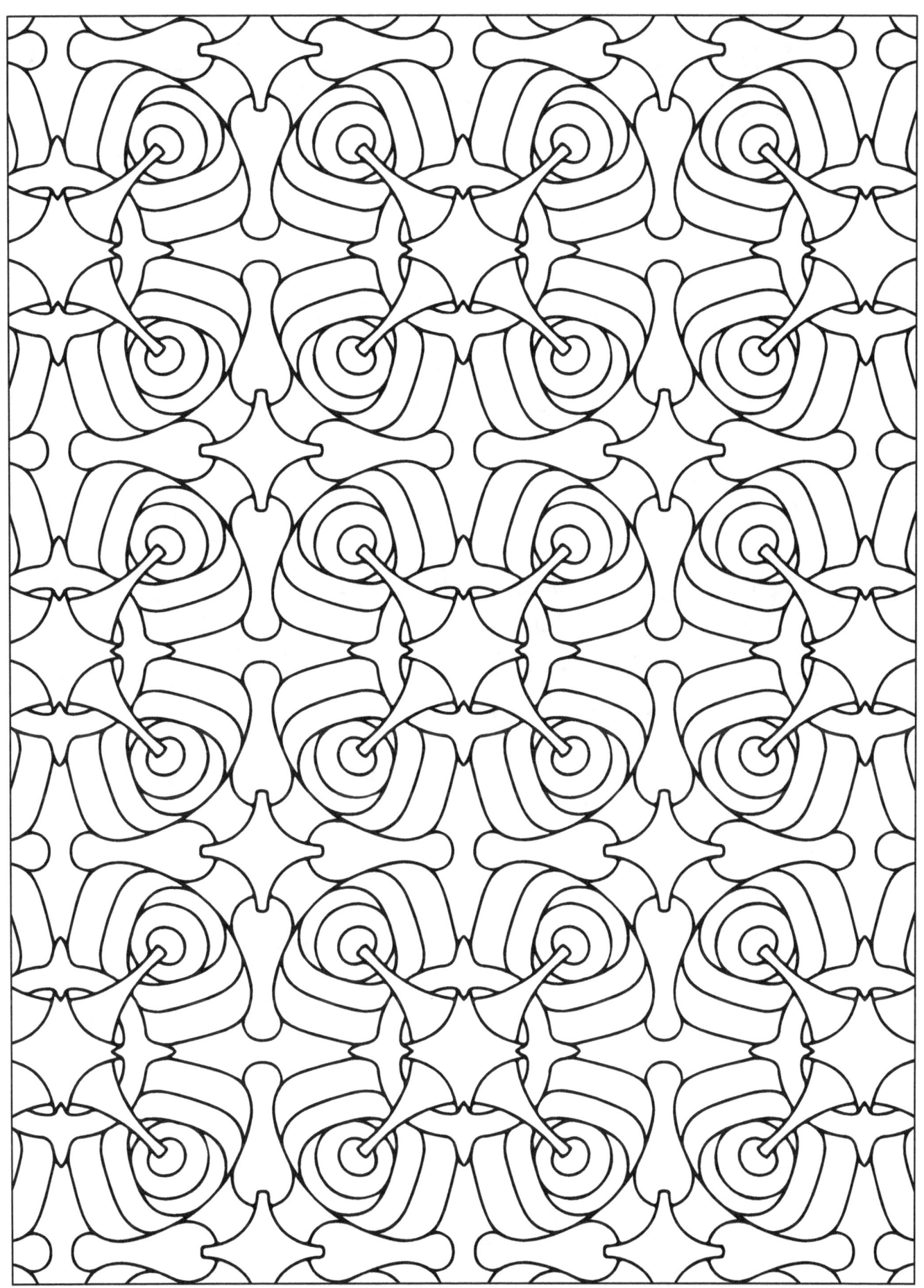

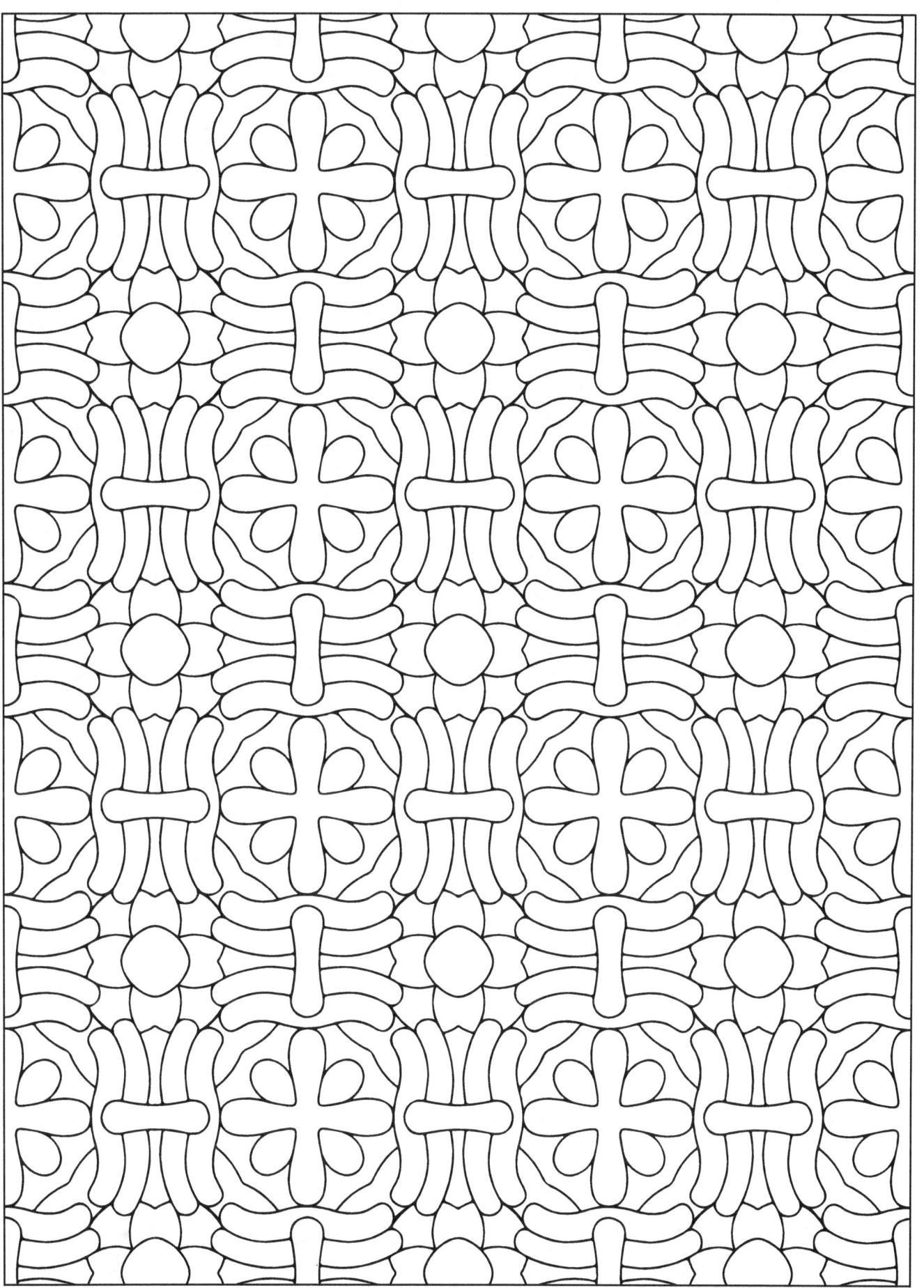

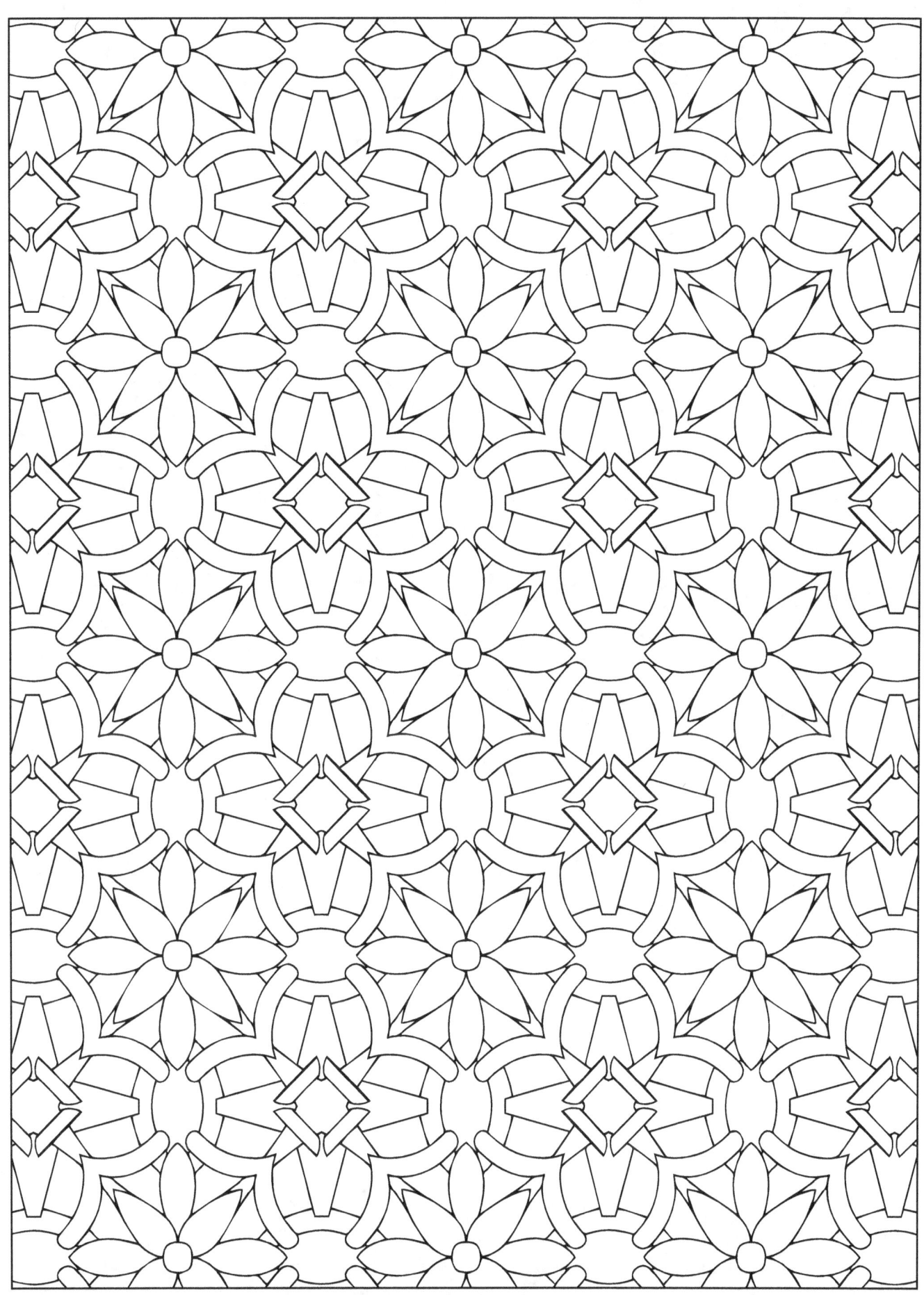

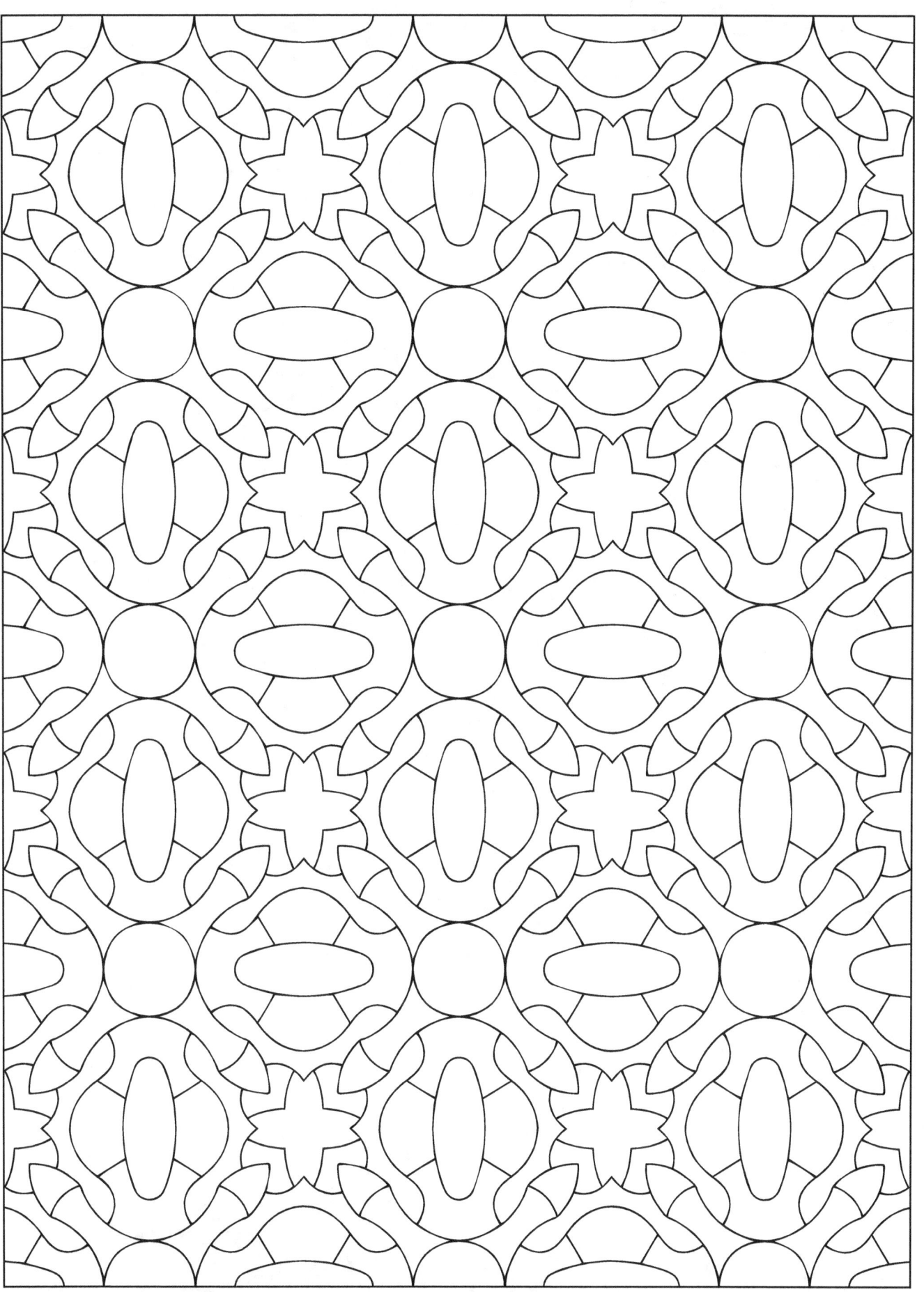

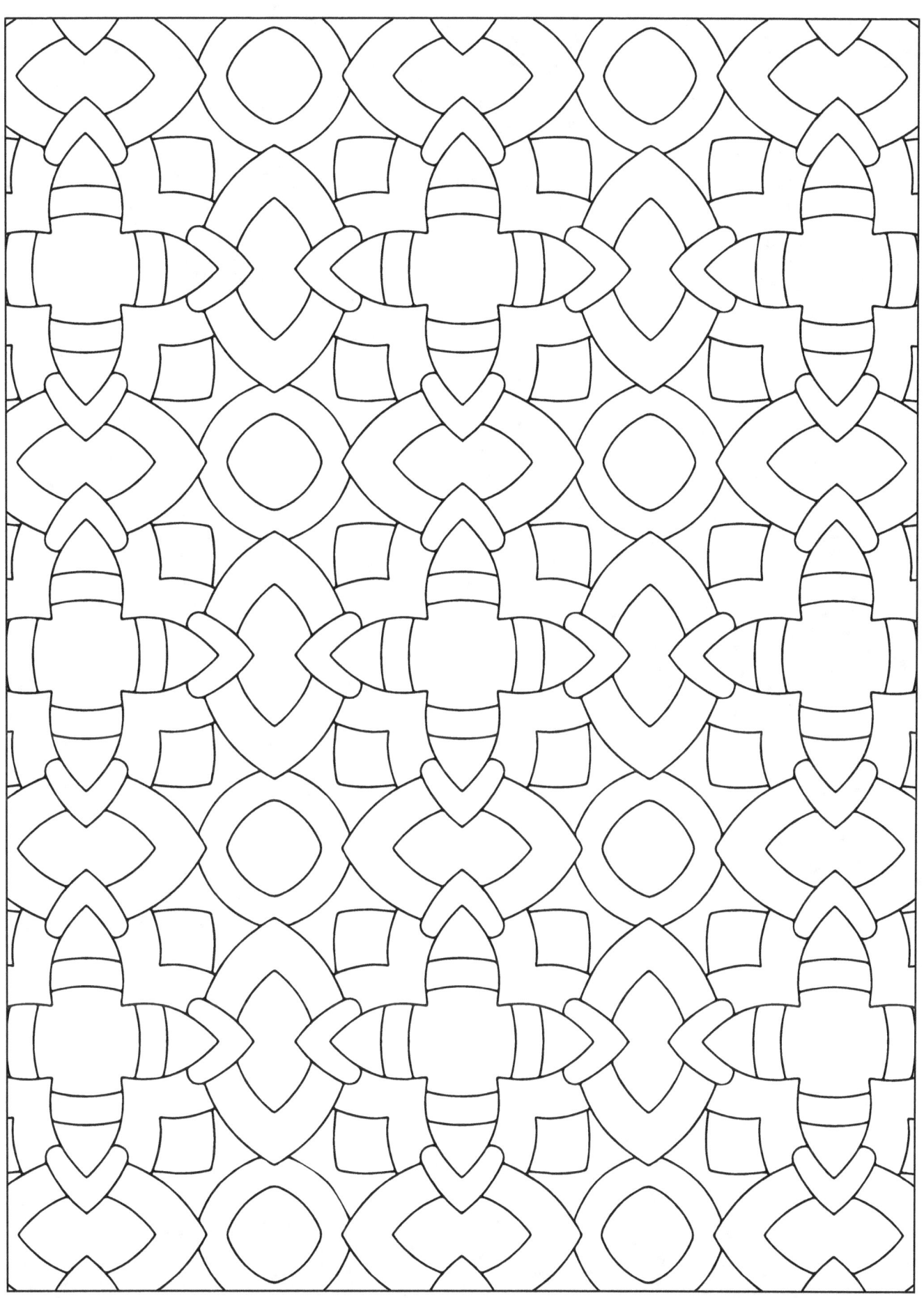

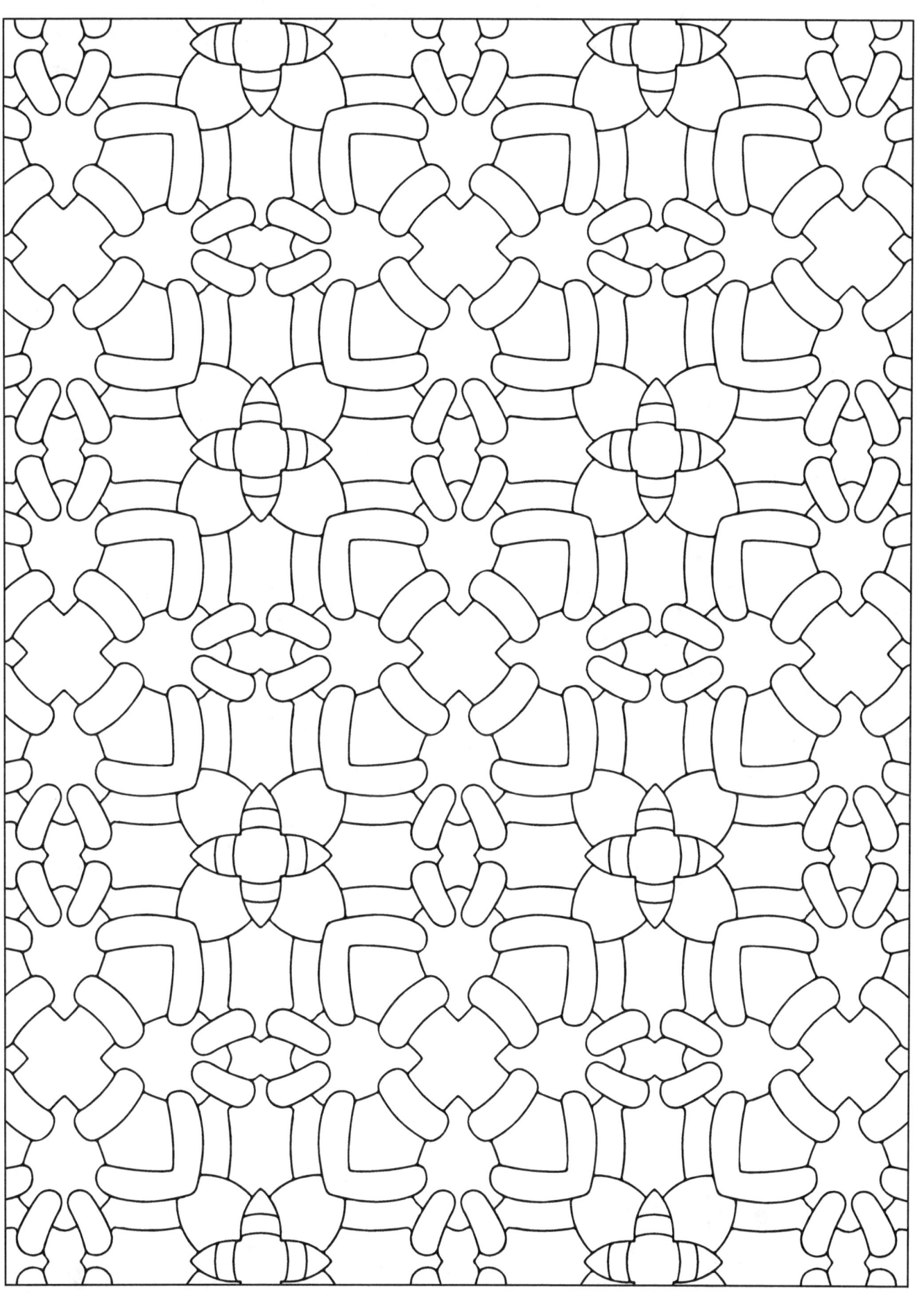

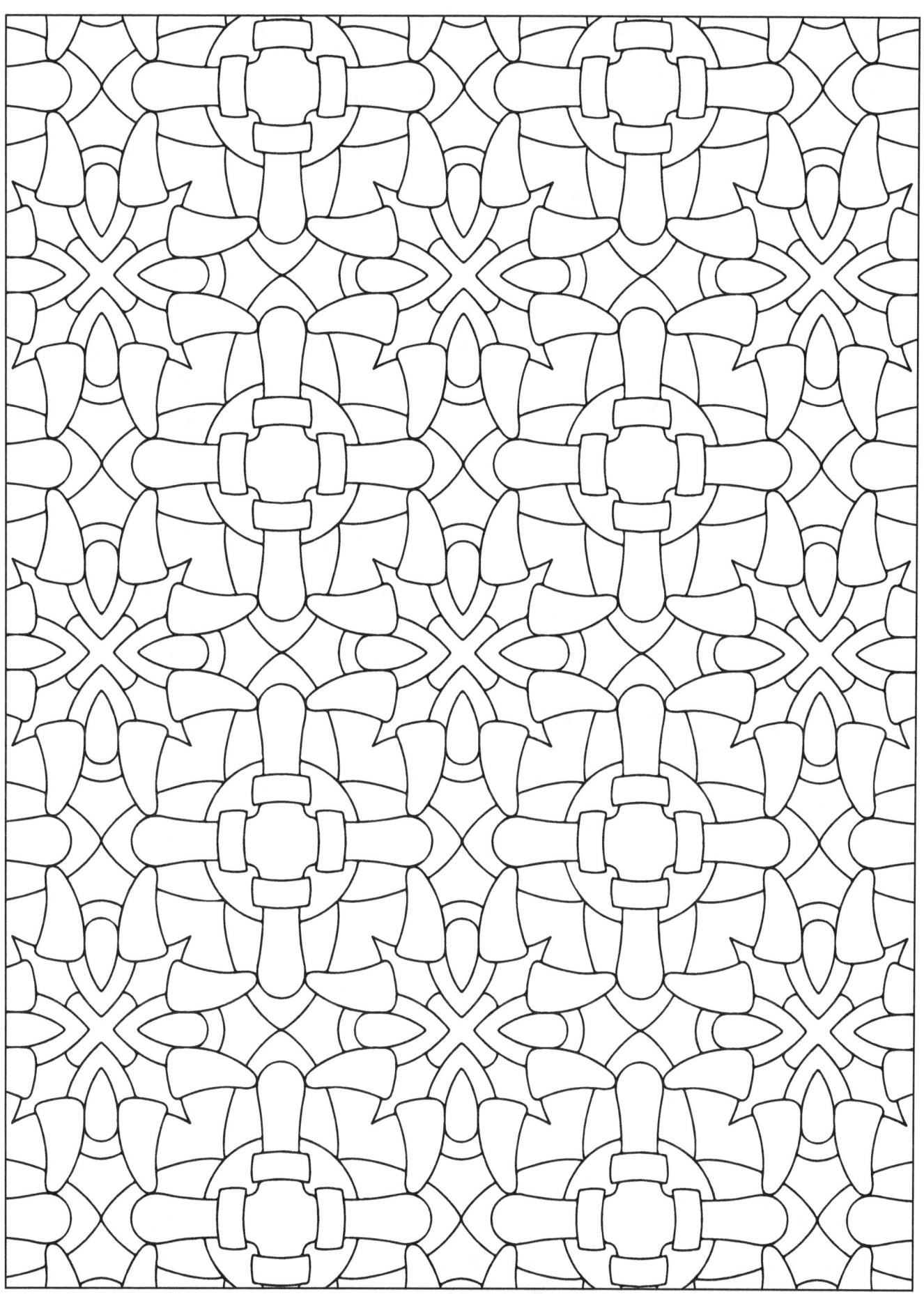

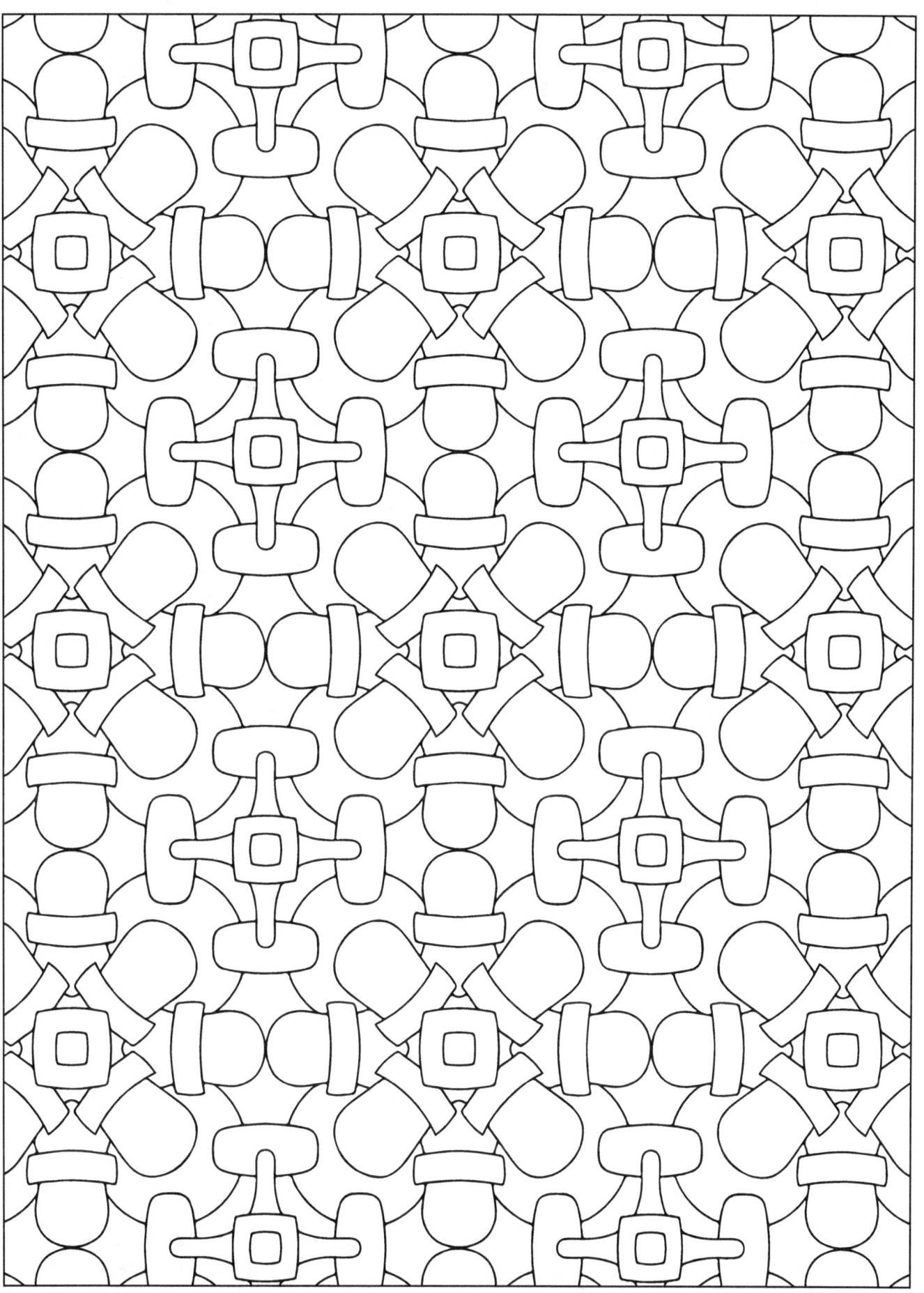

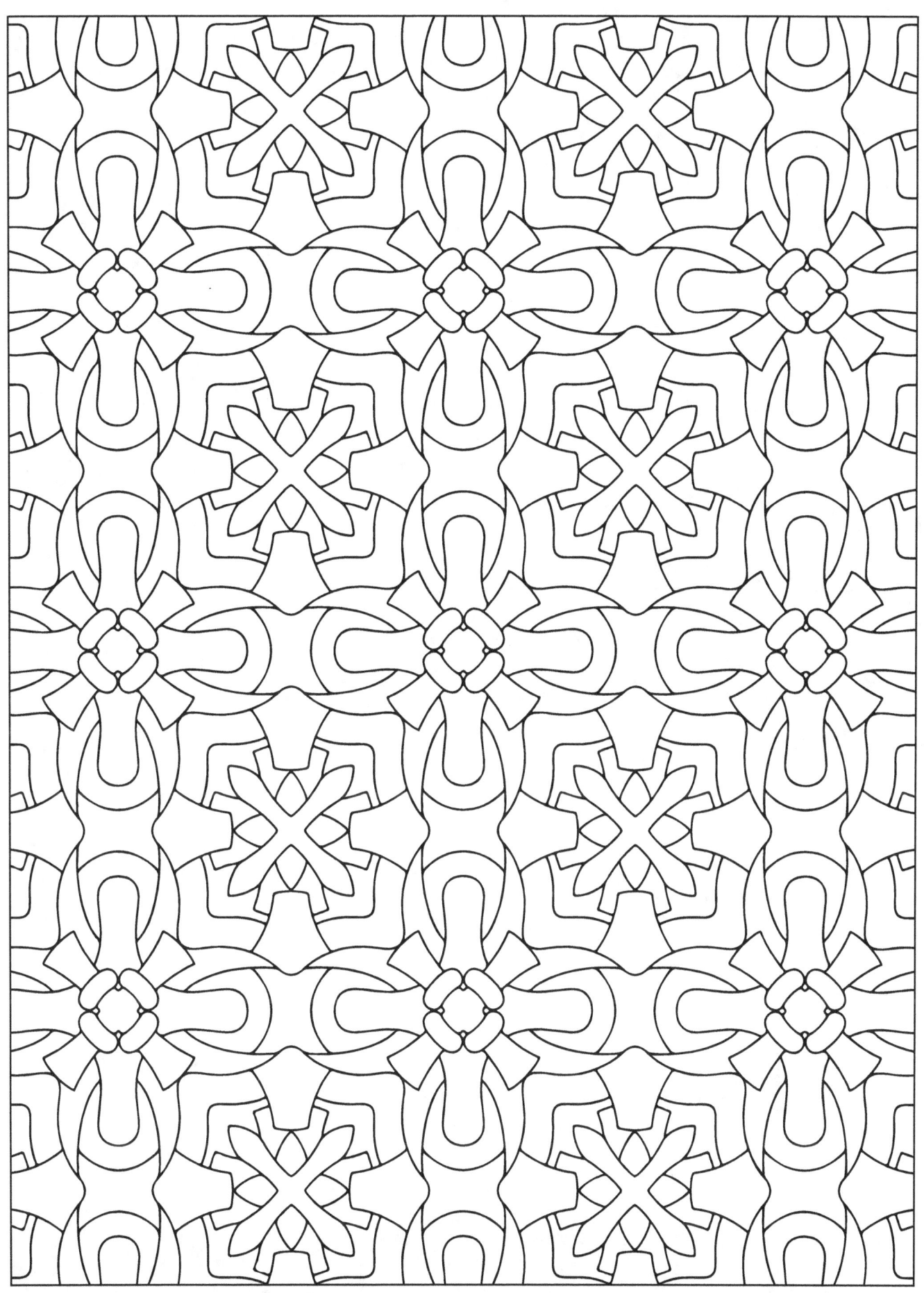

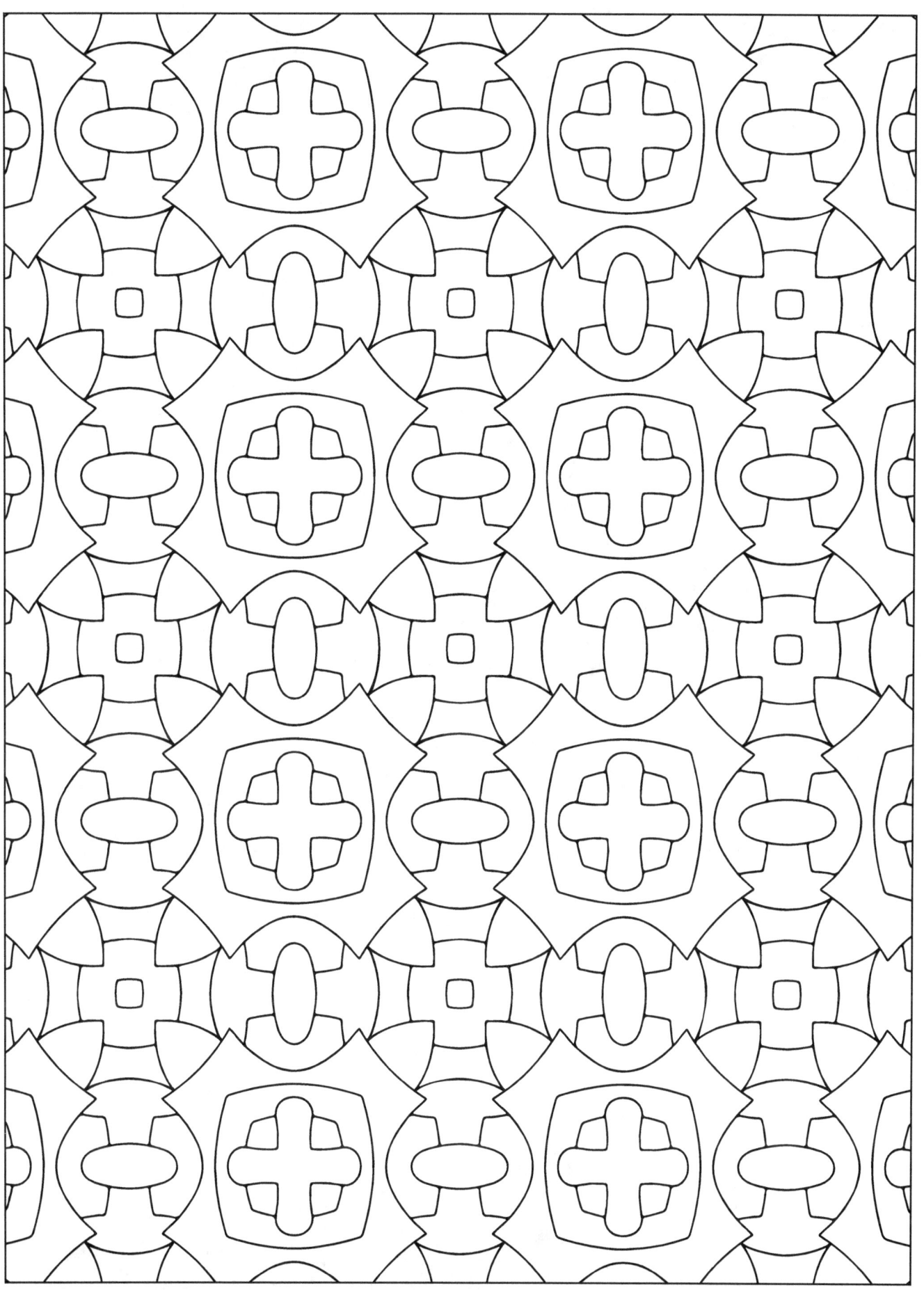

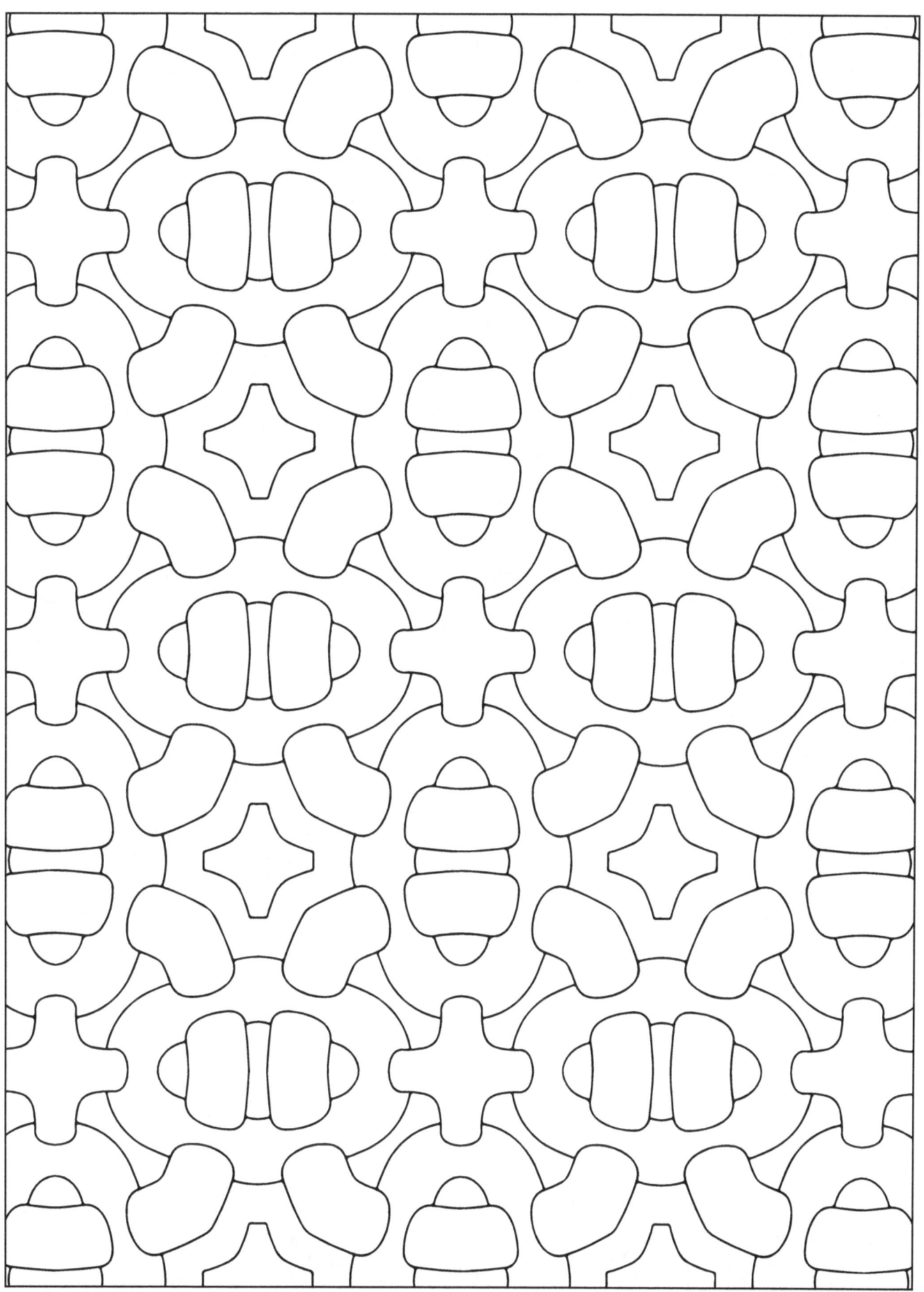

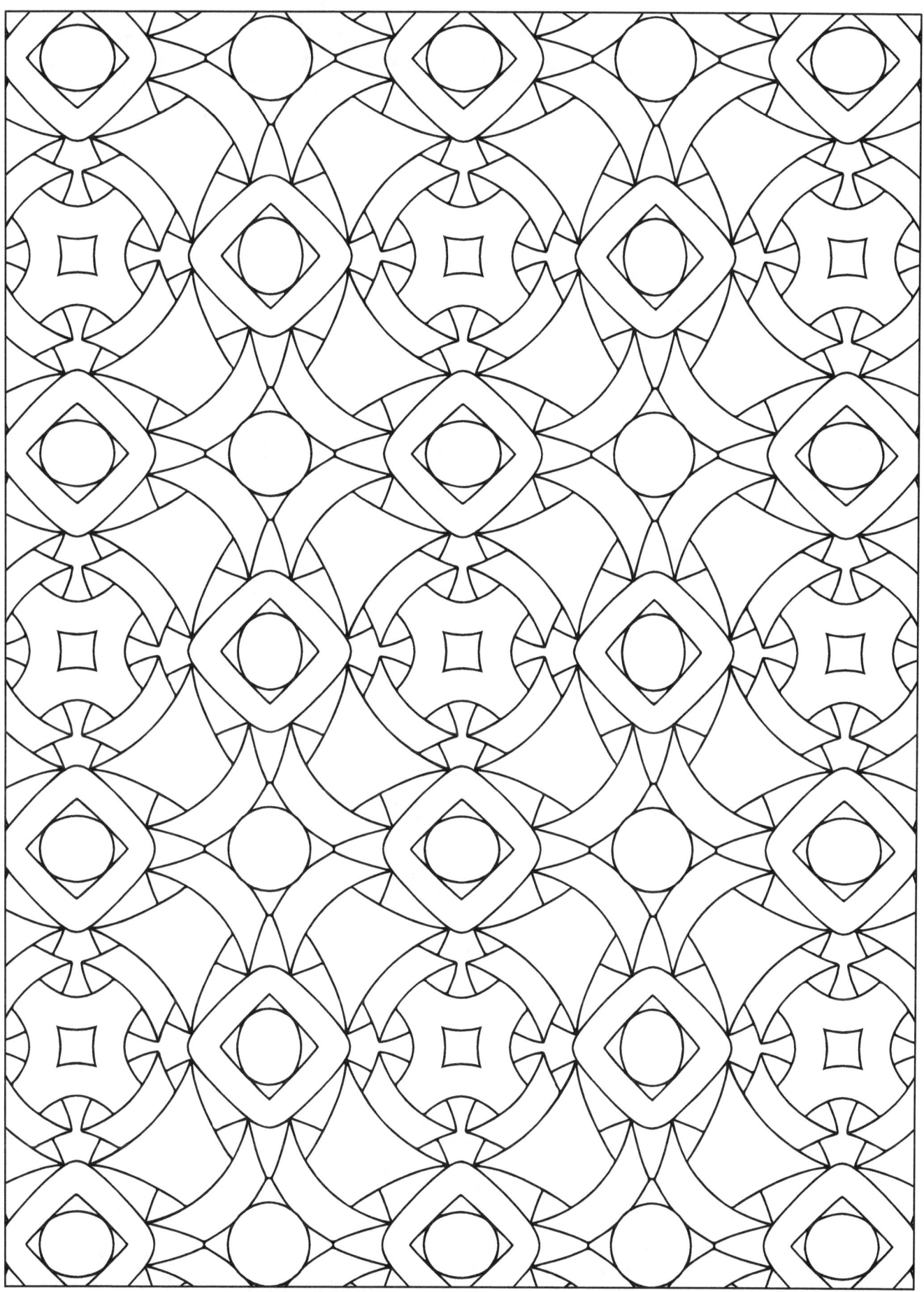

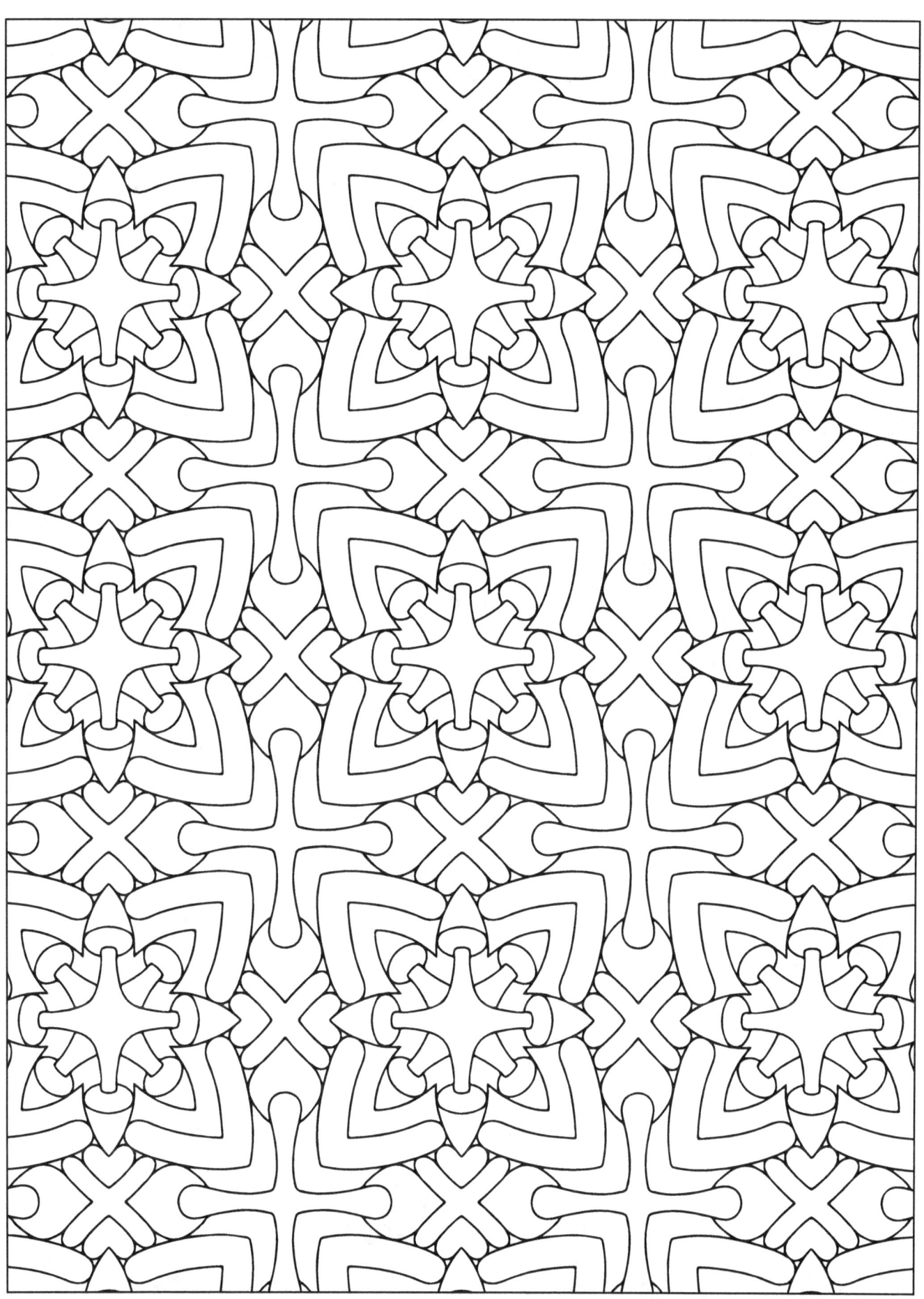

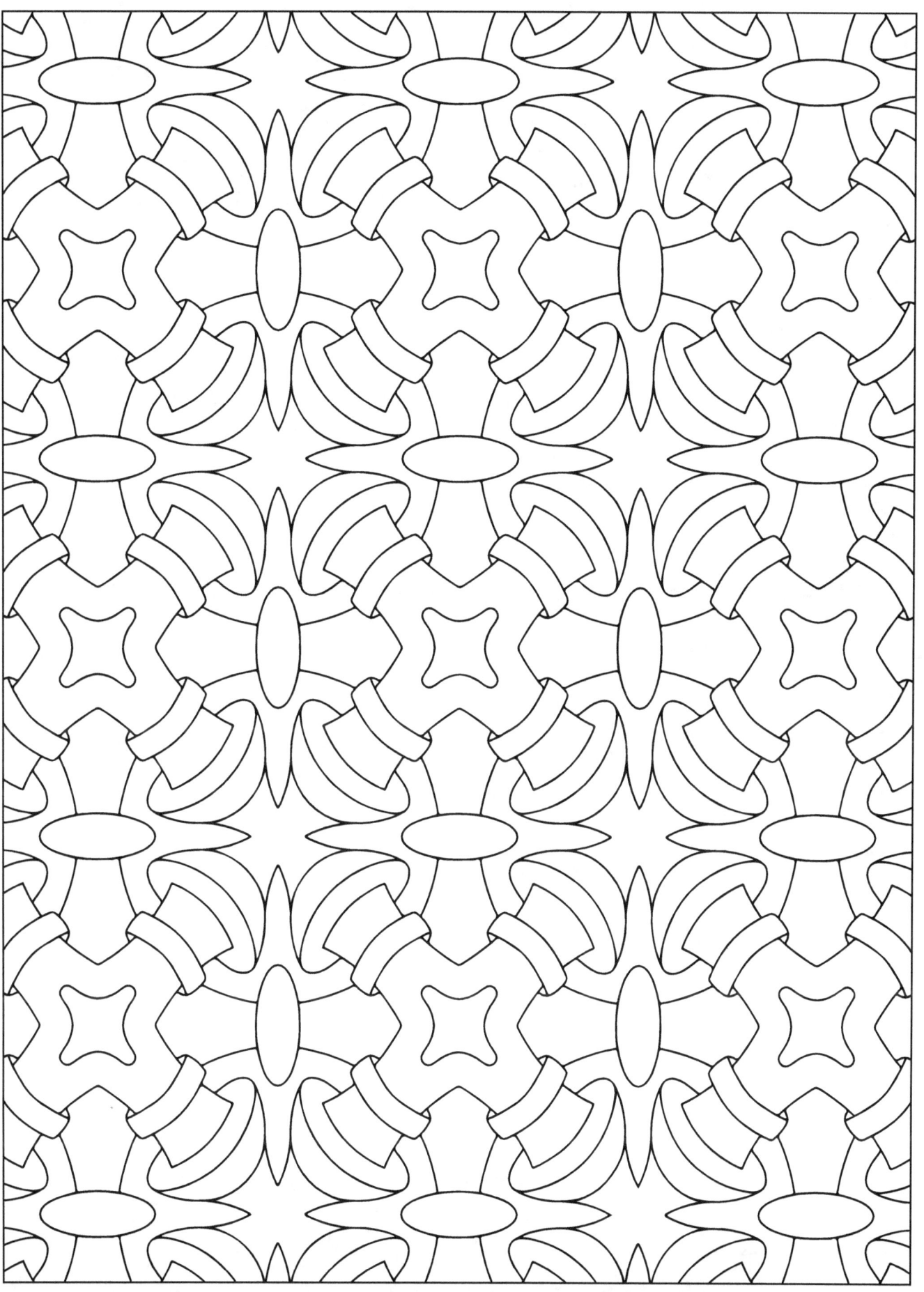

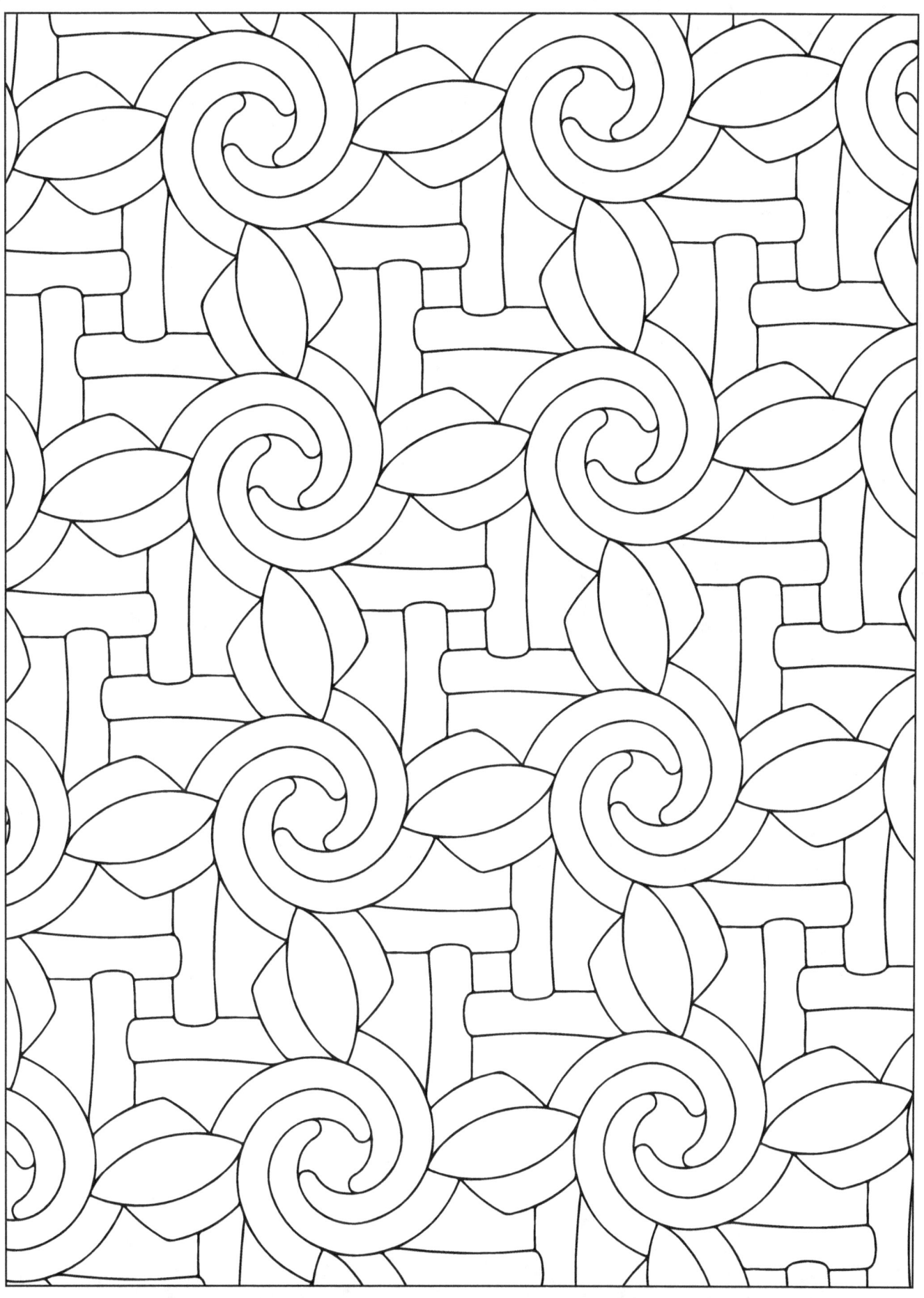

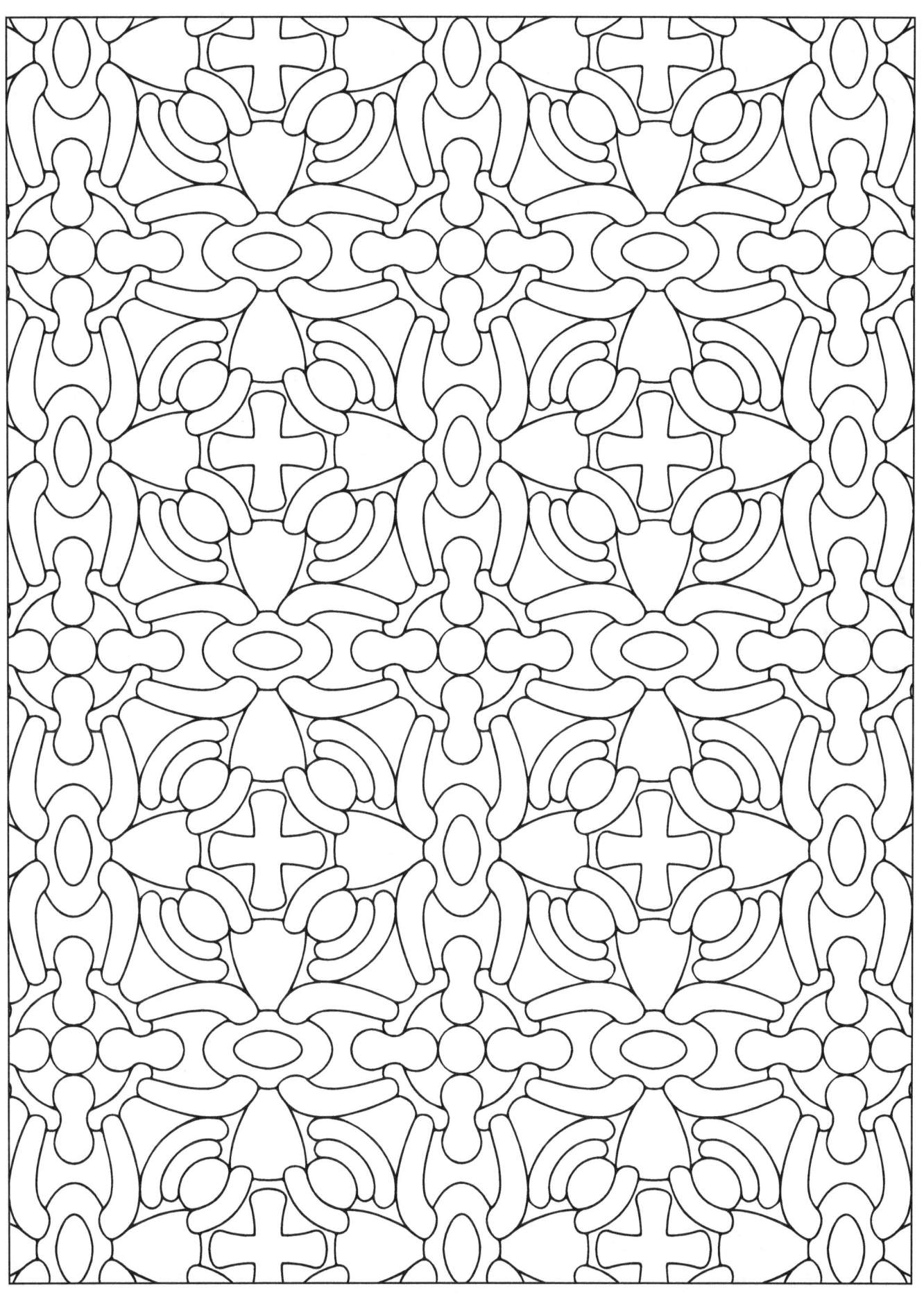

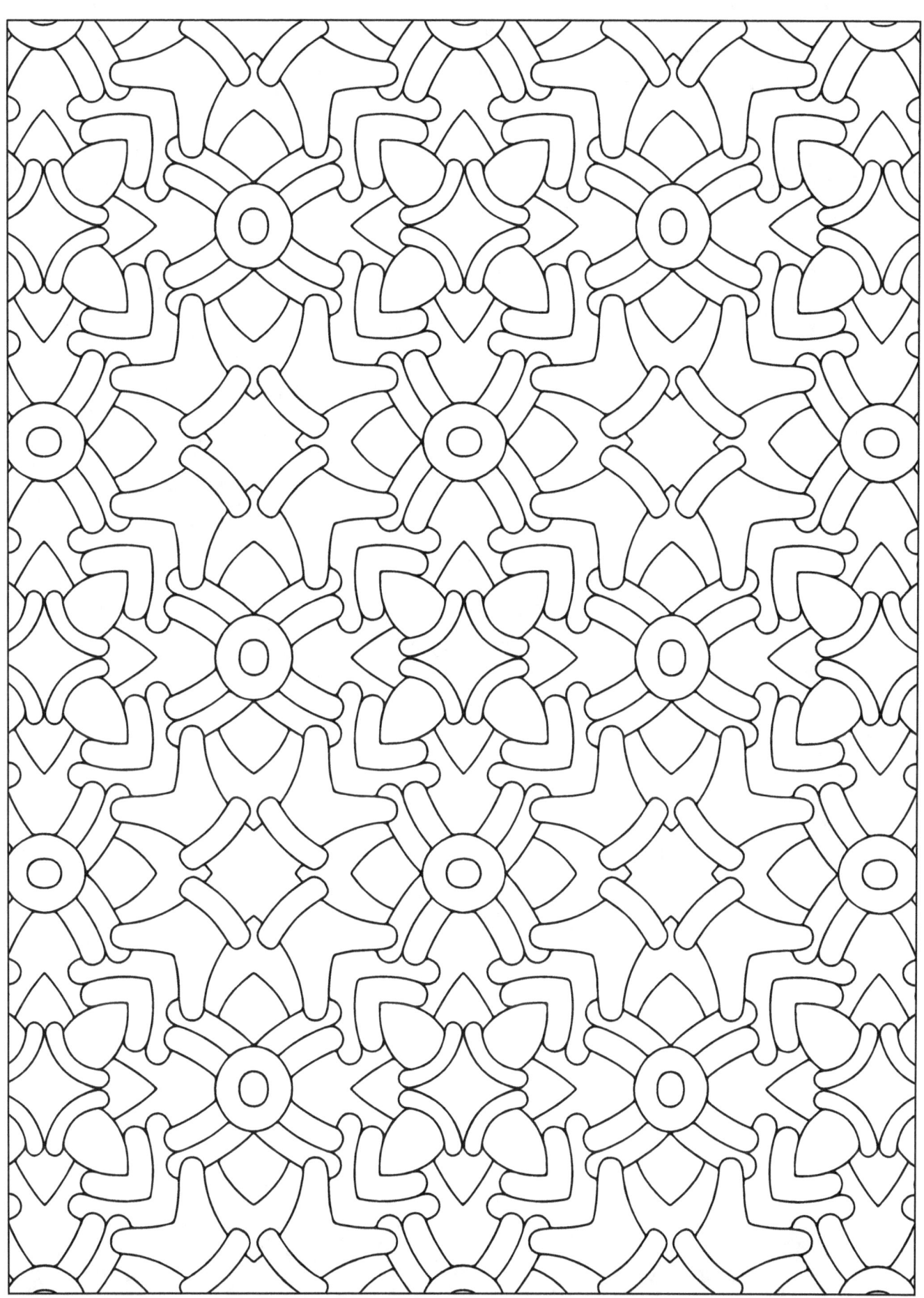

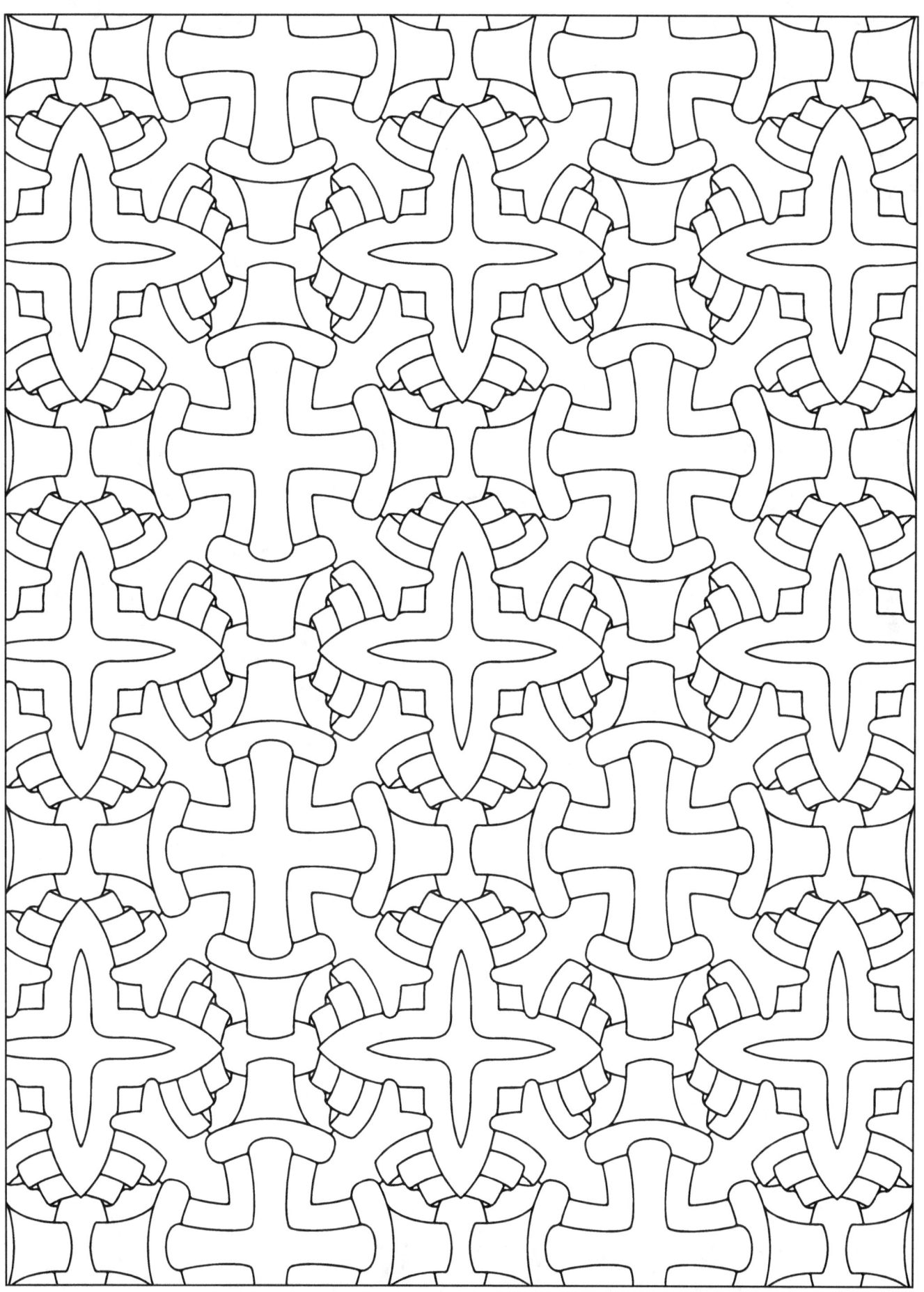

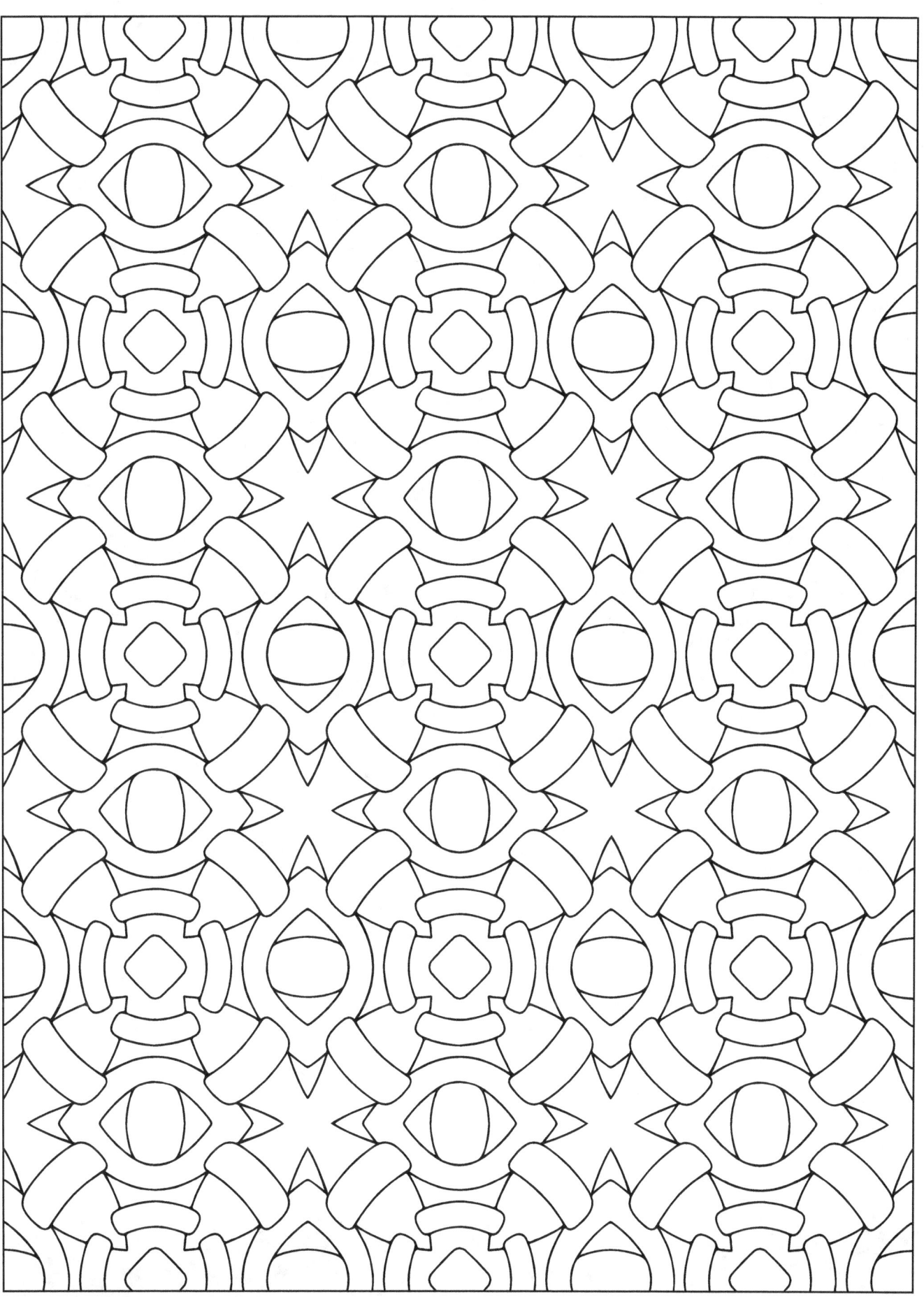

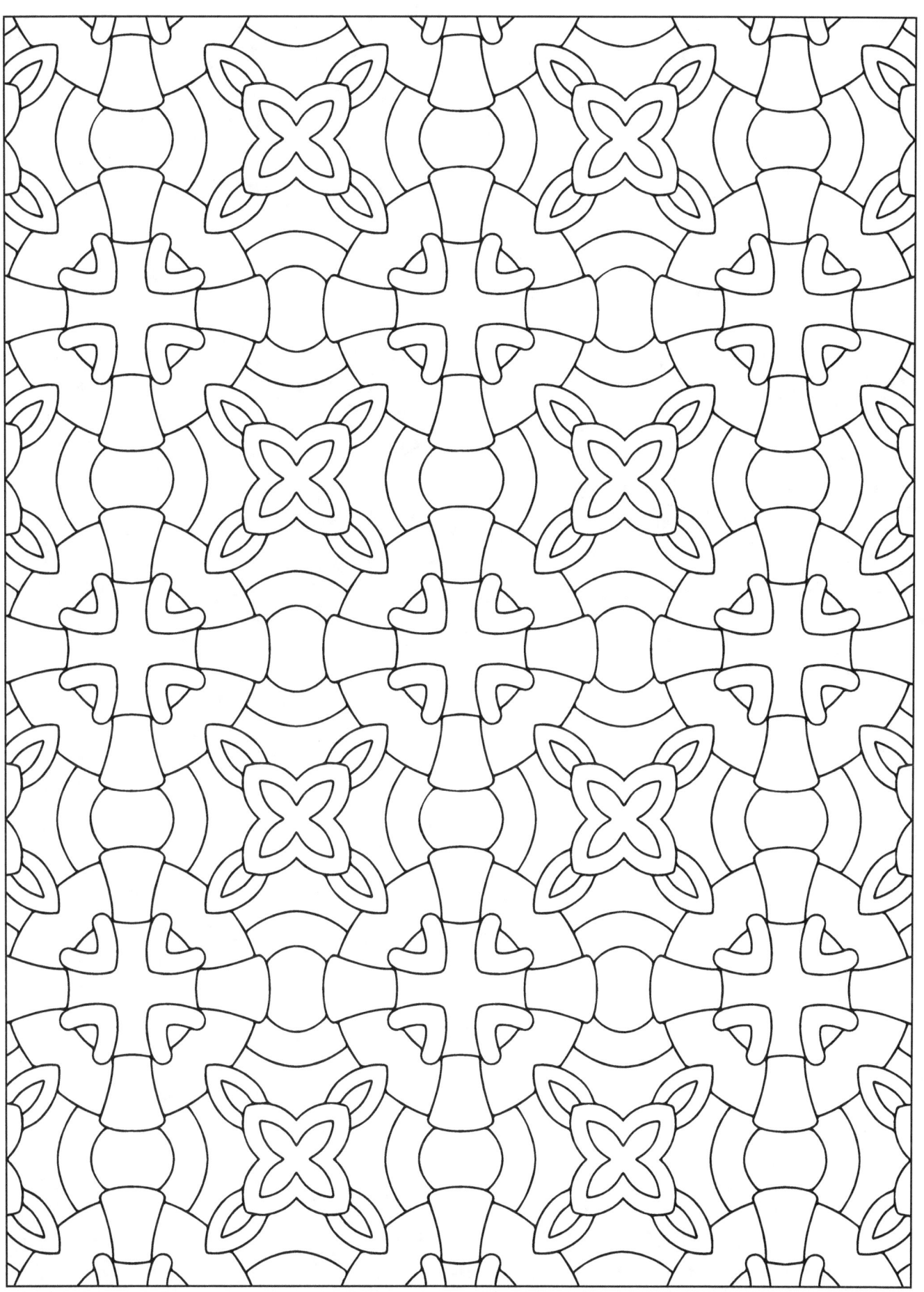

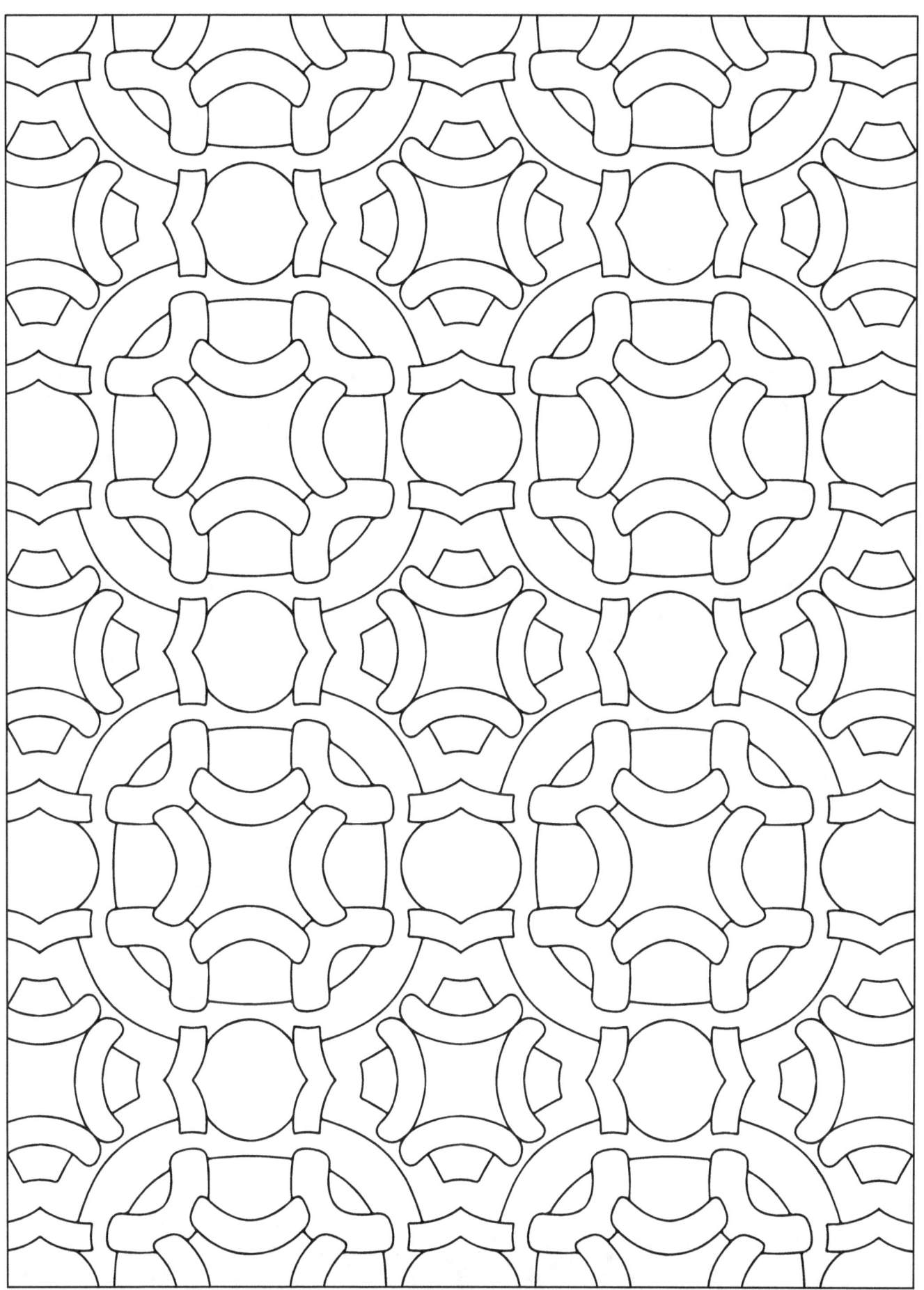

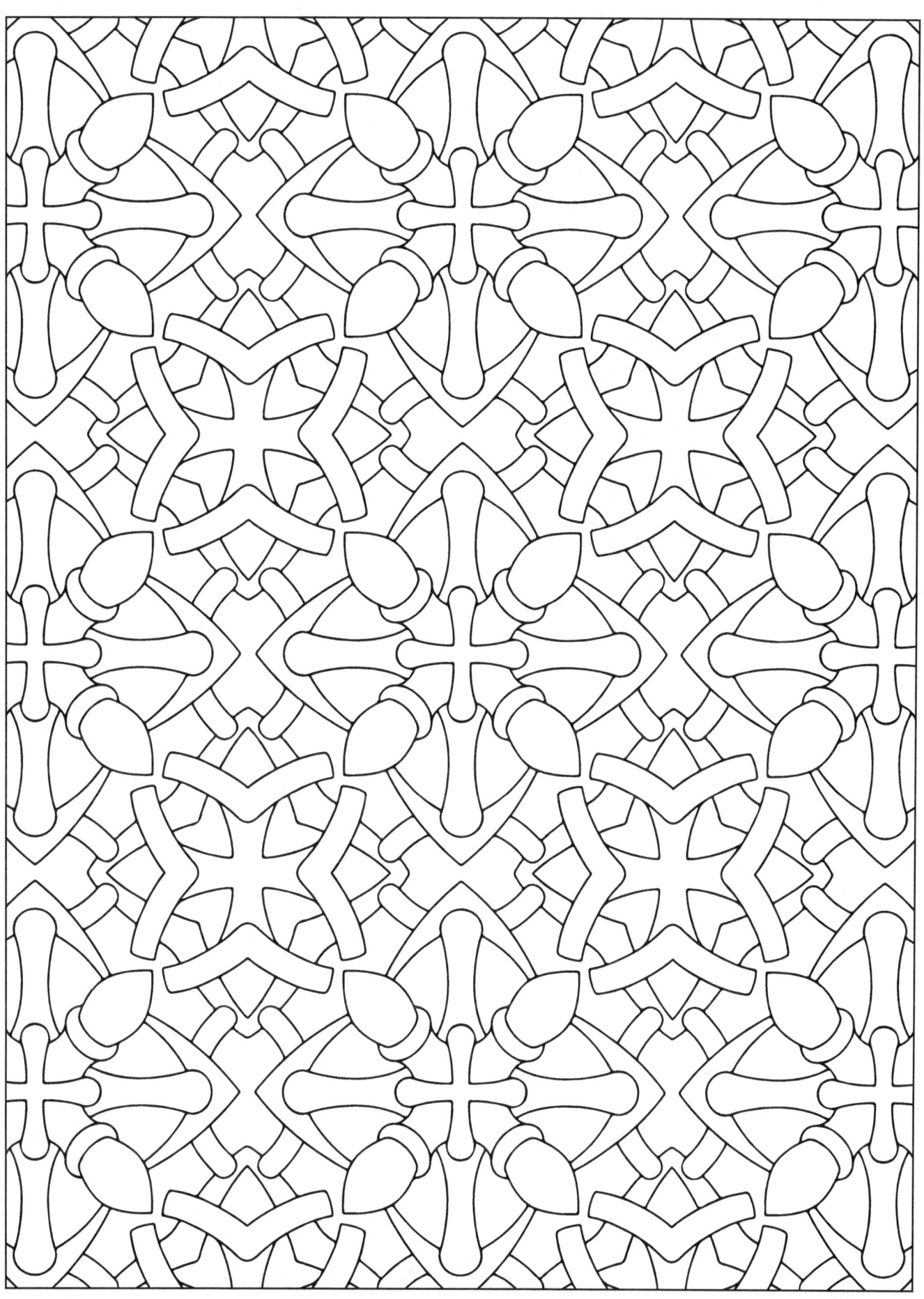

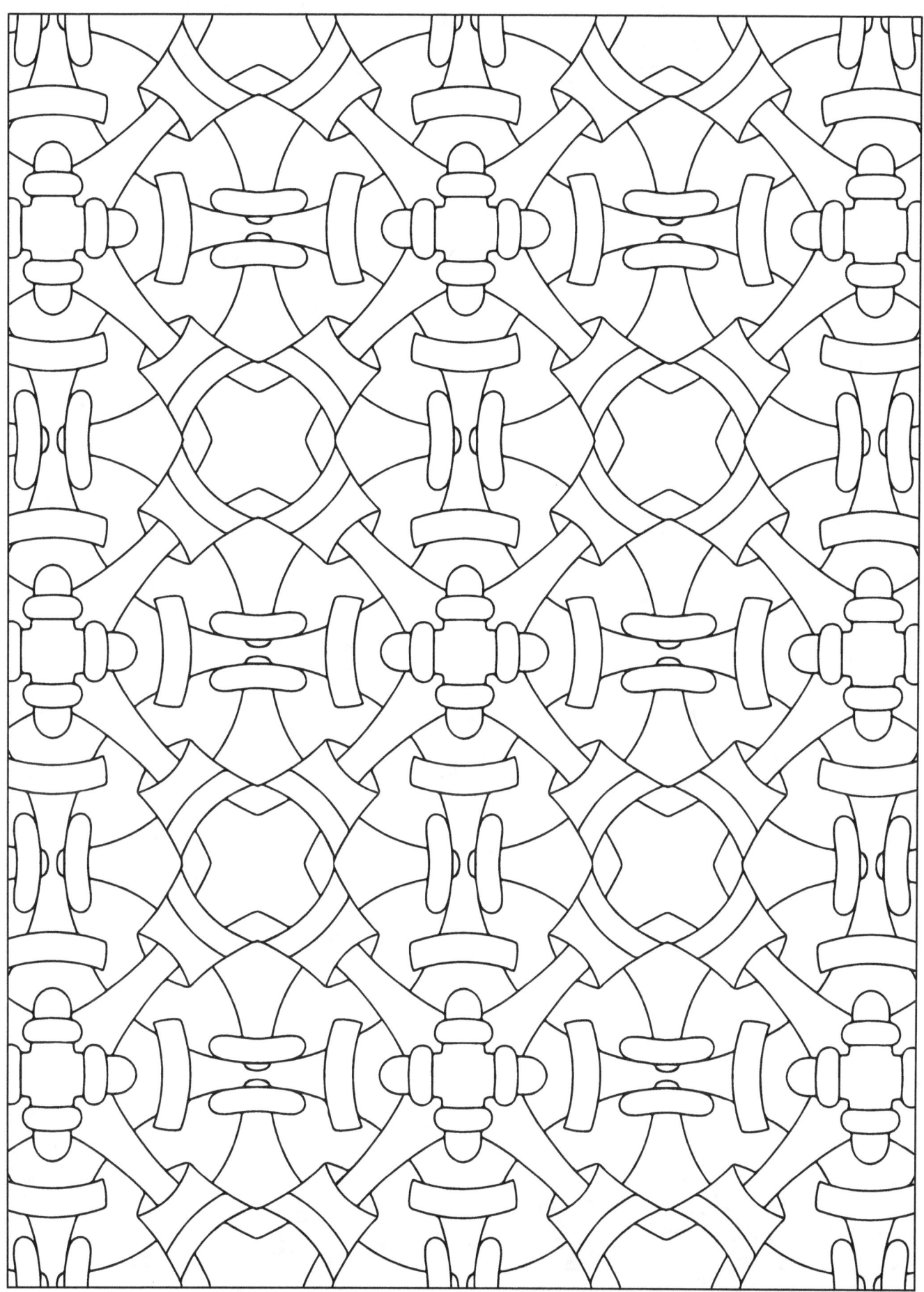

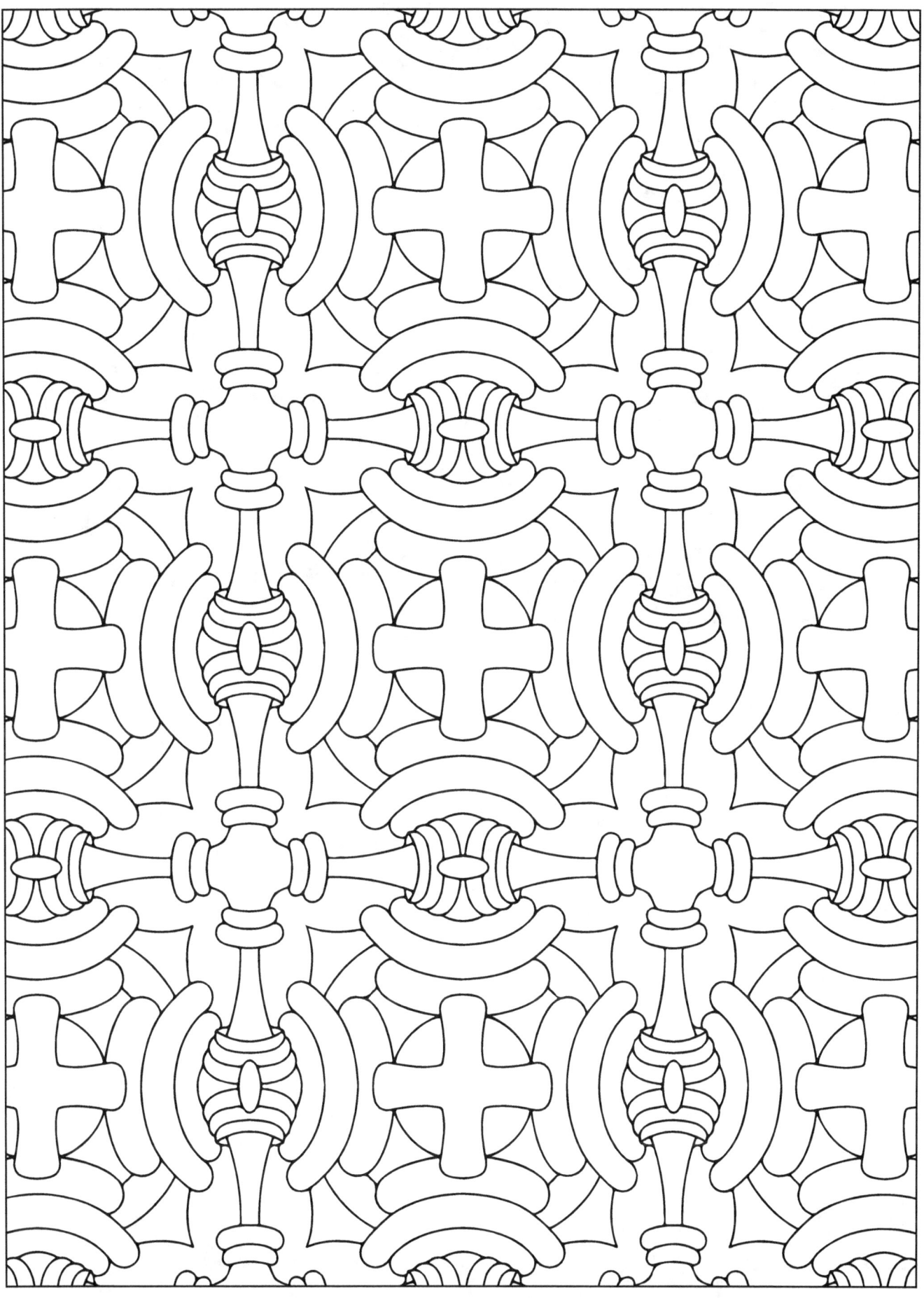

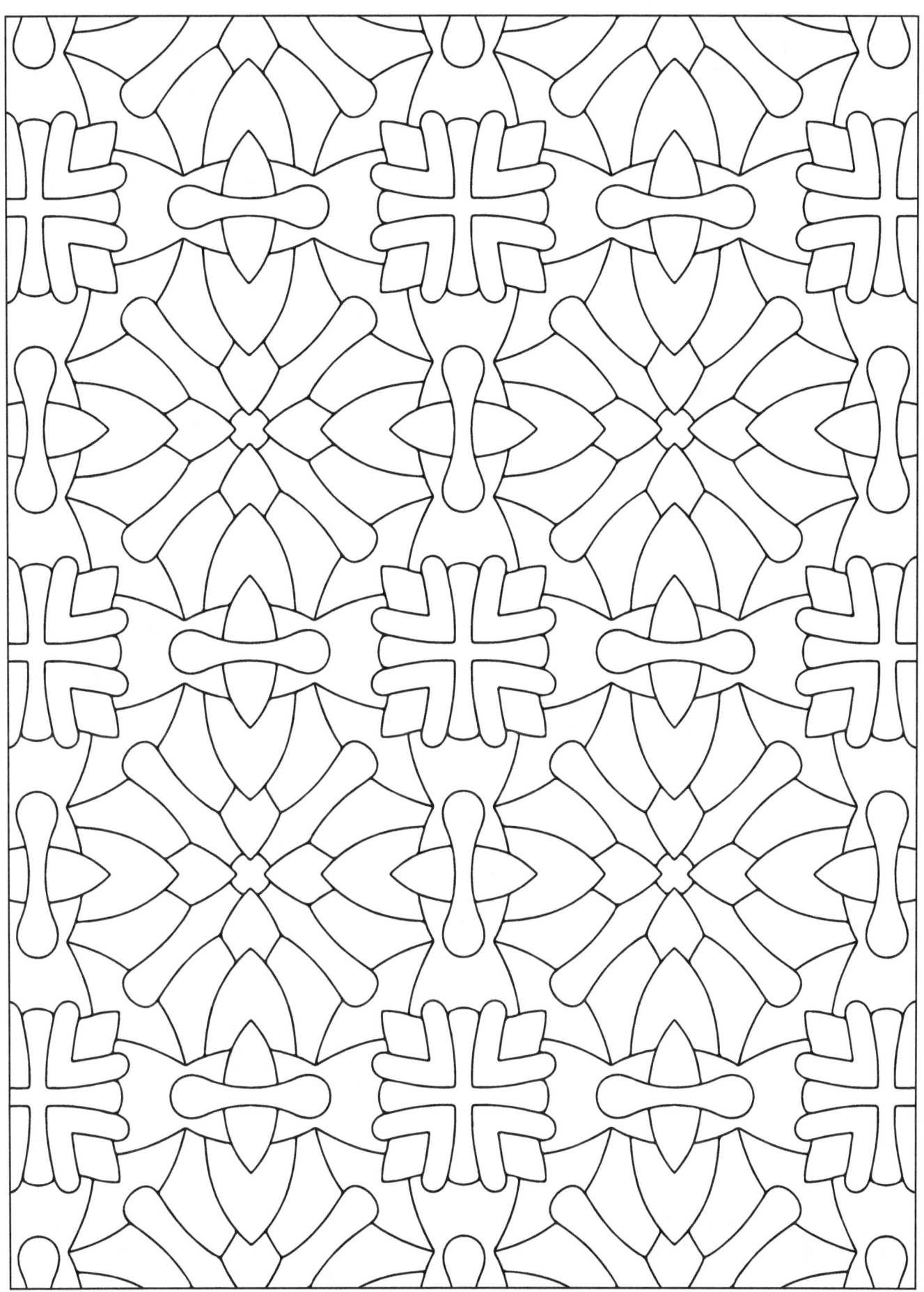

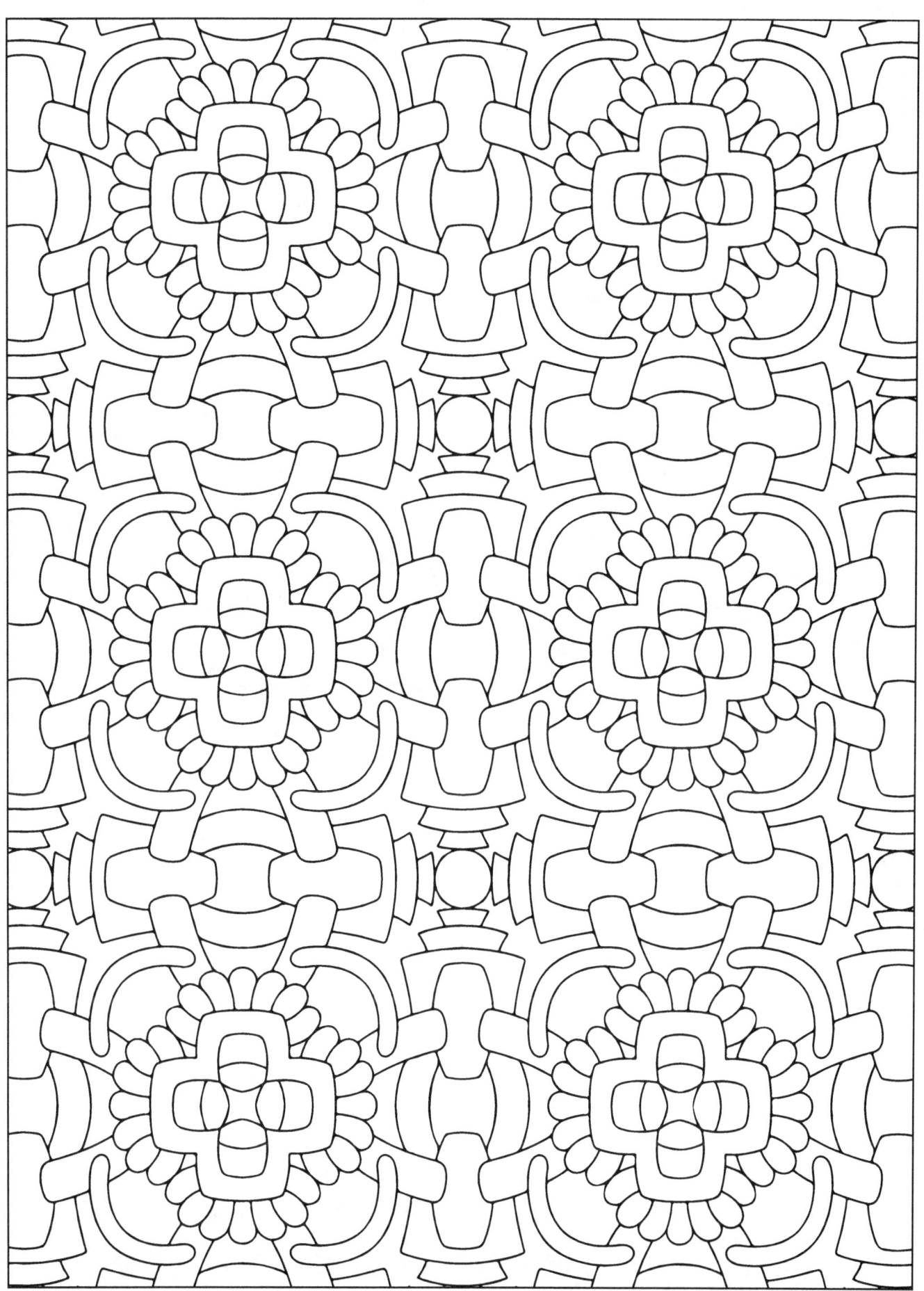

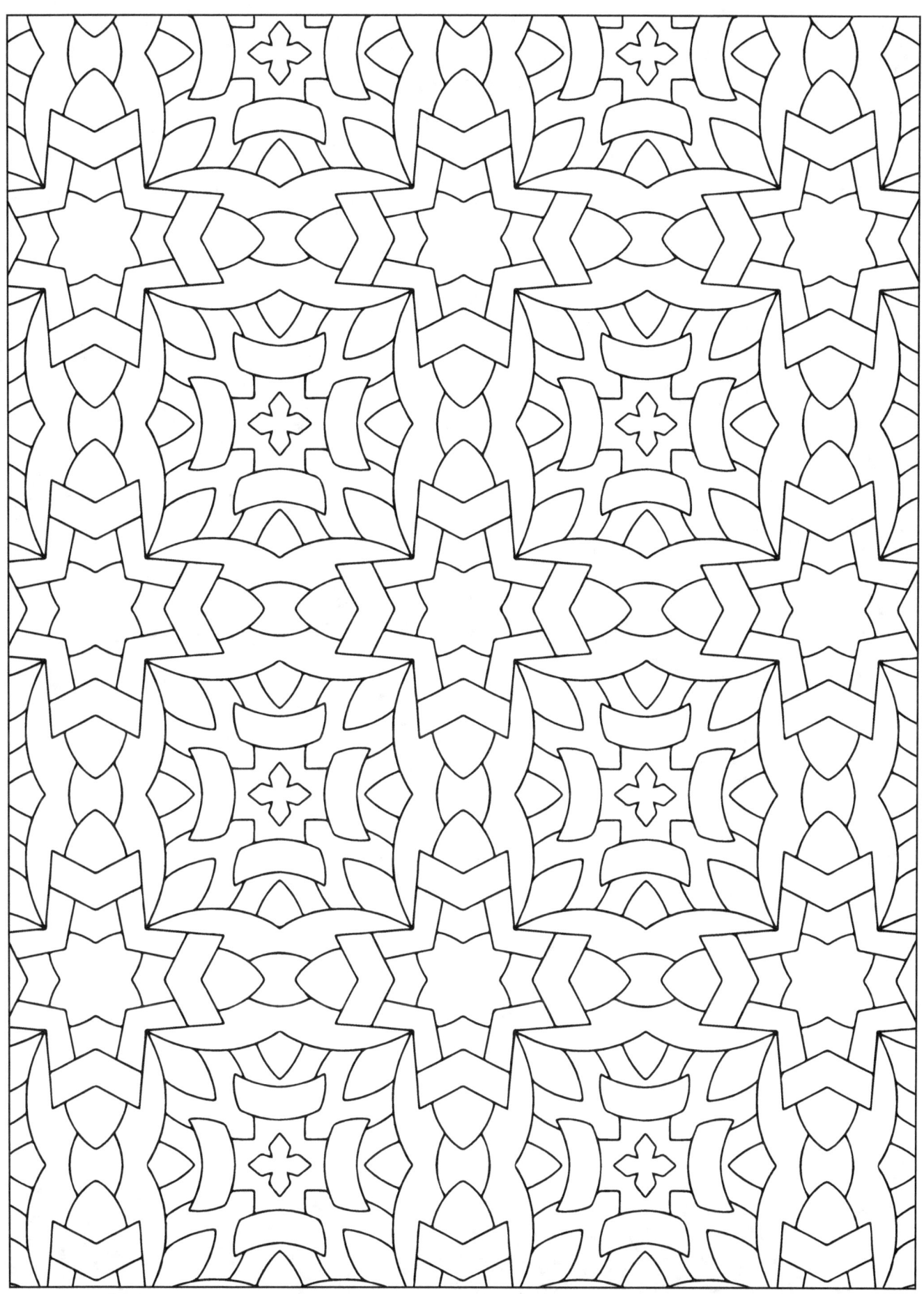

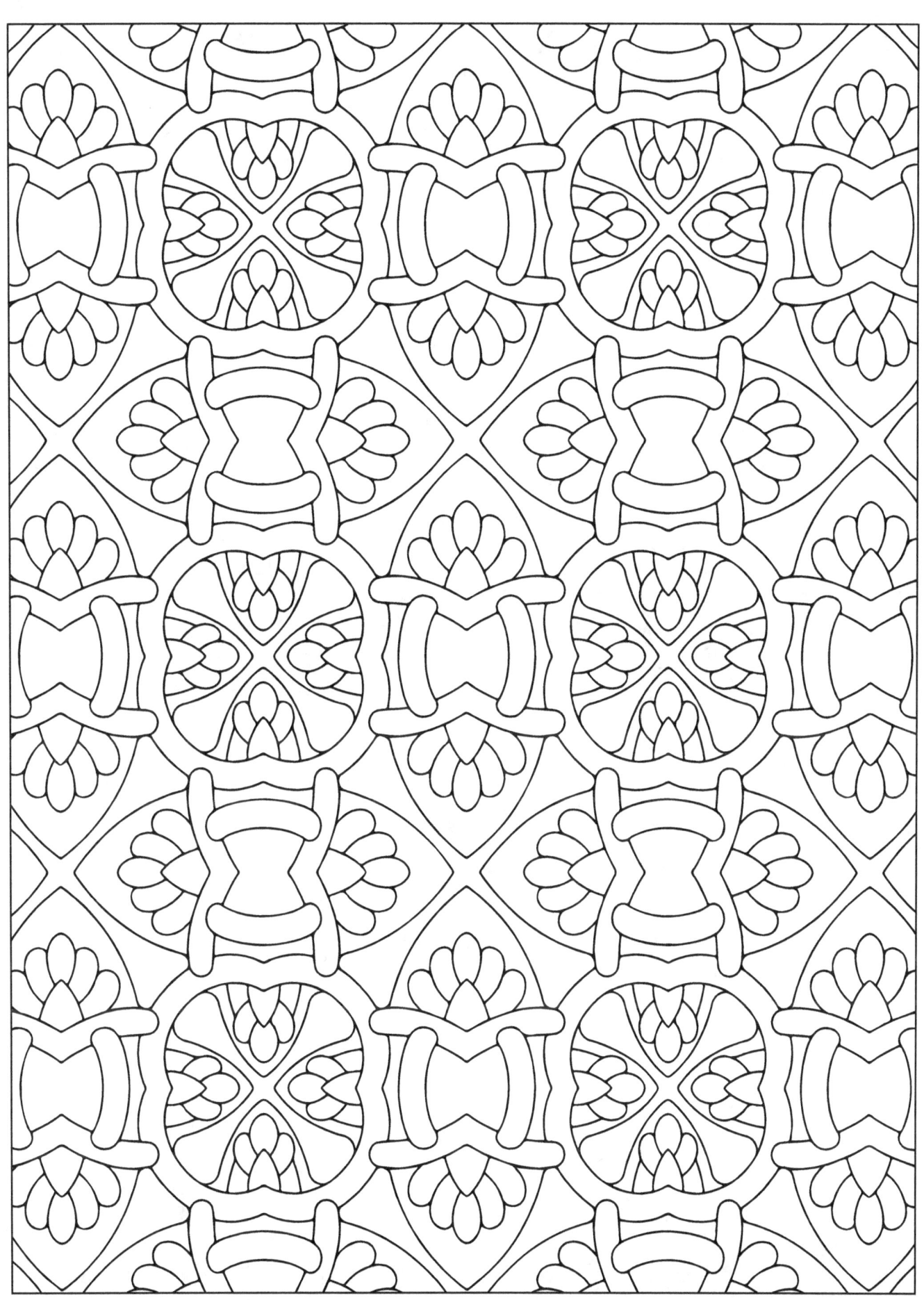

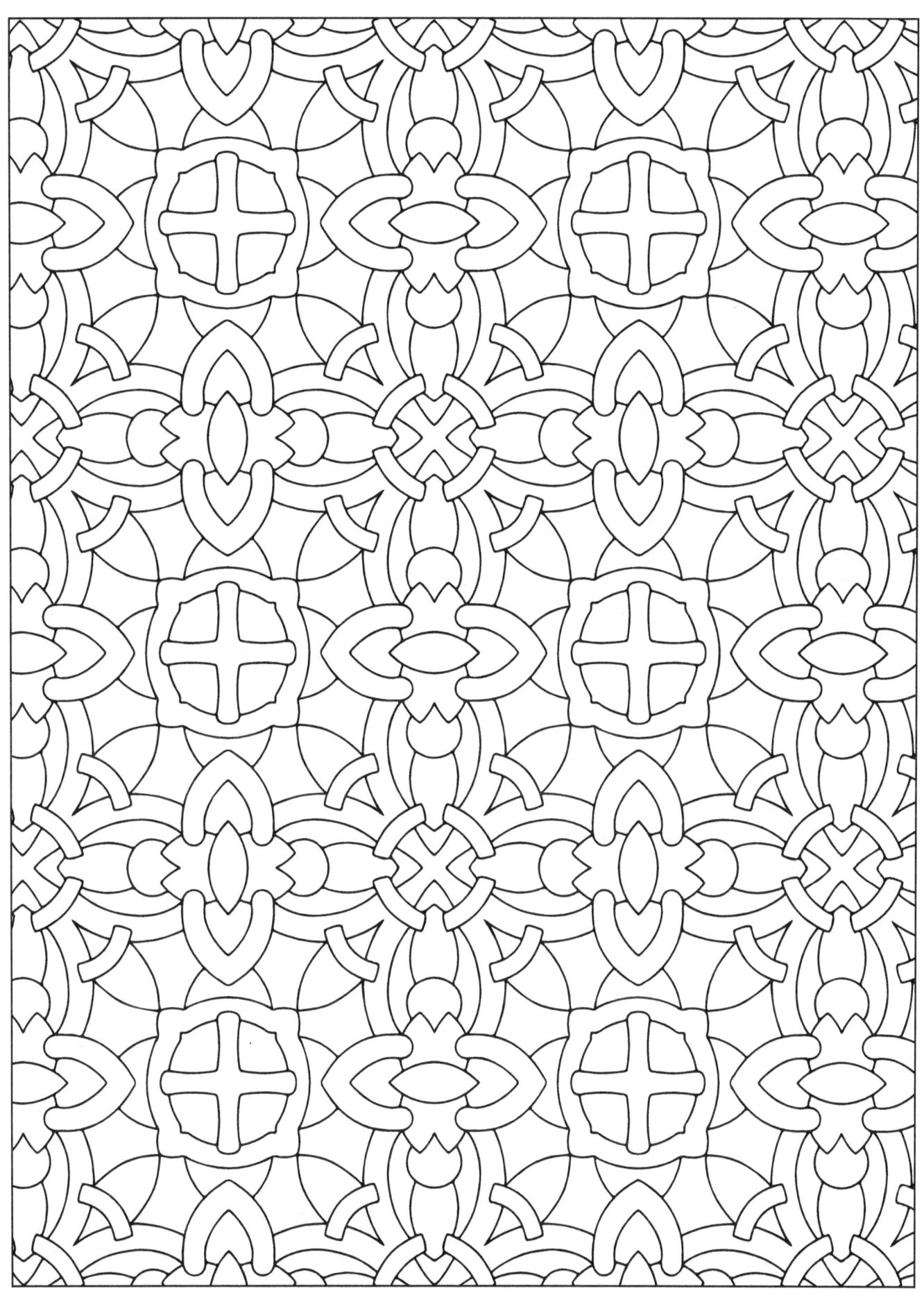

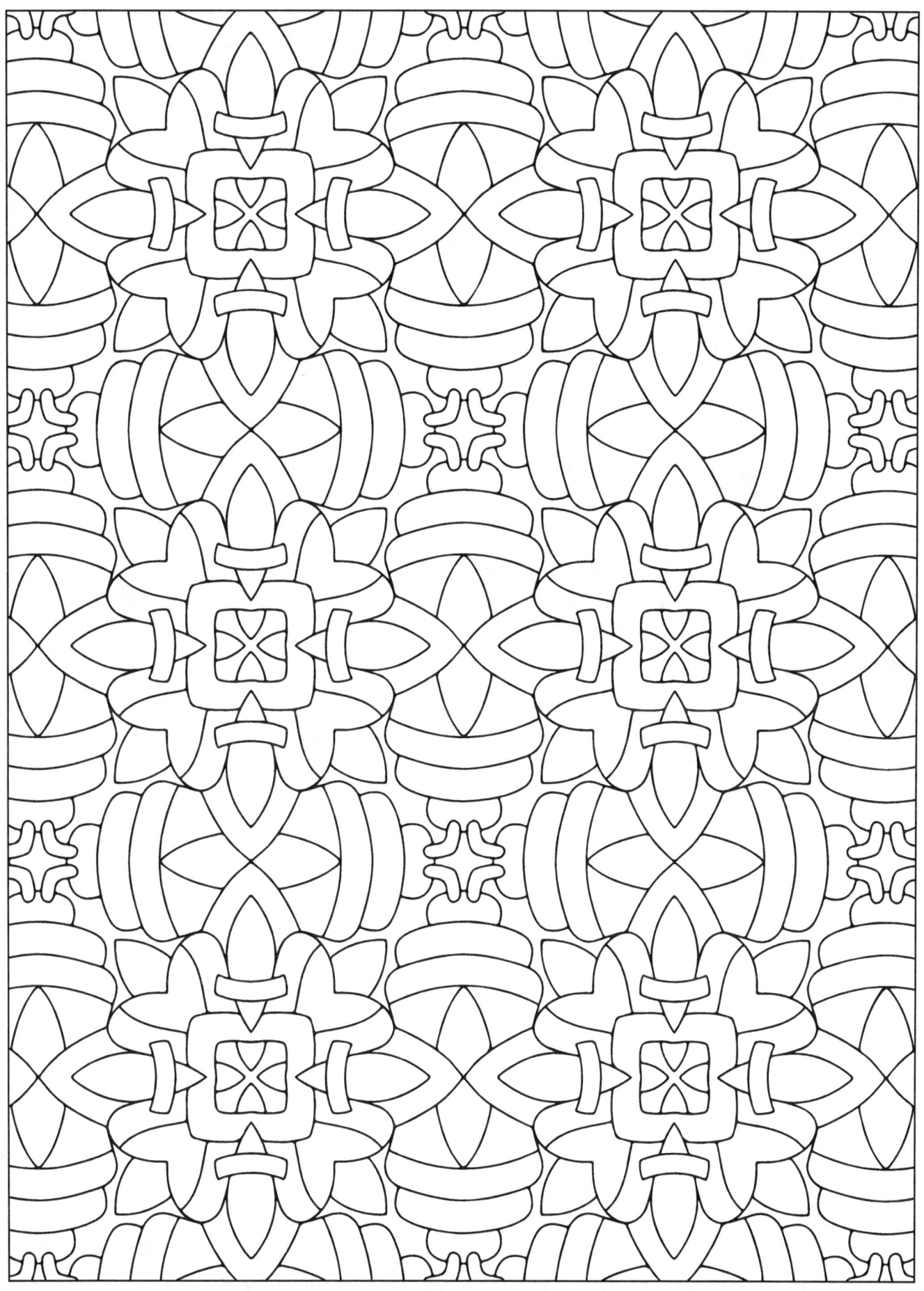

Also by Lori Greenberg

Mandala Coloring Books
Meditative Mandalas - Volume 1
Relaxing Mandalas - Volume 2
Calming Mandalas - Volume 3
Fanciful Mandalas - Volume 4

Pattern Coloring Books
Meditative Patterns - Volume 1
Relaxing Patterns - Volume 2
Calming Patterns - Volume 3

Pocket Pattern Coloring Books
Pocket Patterns - Volume 1

Large Space Pattern Coloring Books
Easy Patterns - Volume 1

Affirmation Coloring Books
Meditative Affirmations - Volume 1

Find these, and future books on Amazon

Visit **www.lorigreenberg.com**
and join Lori Greenberg's Coloring Connection
Facebook group for free coloring pages
and updates on new books.